Making Inclusion Work for Children with Dyspraxia

This book gives the reader a unique insight and understanding of the hidden disability – dyspraxia. Drawing on considerable experience of the condition, as well as current research findings, the authors help teachers and other education and health professionals to genuinely appreciate the needs of a child with dyspraxia. Through the implementation of practical strategies, they show how teachers can make all the differences to a child's ability to succeed in the classroom, and demonstrate through case studies how parents, teachers and therapists can work together to facilitate learning.

While providing a comprehensive overview of dyspraxia, this lively, informative text also examines specific cases and scenarios, considering the perspective of teachers and parents, and those surrounding the child. It handles a range of crucial topics such as:

- issues surrounding diagnosis;
- the developmental differences and characteristics of dyspraxia;
- intervention strategies in line with the National Curriculum;
- barriers to inclusion;
- an exploration of the pressures on families;
- ways of improving home–school liaison.

Teachers, Special Educational Needs Coordinators and health professionals will find this book provides a wealth of essential information and guidance, while parents will also find much to support them in the daily care and welfare of their child.

Gill Dixon is an Independent Educational Inclusion/Dyspraxia Adviser and Trainer and a lecturer, and has a son with dyspraxia. **Lois M. Addy** is Senior Lecturer at the School of Professional Health Studies, York St John College.

Making Inclusion Work for Children with Dyspraxia

Practical strategies for teachers

Gill Dixon and Lois M. Addy

Routledge
Taylor & Francis Group

LONDON AND NEW YORK

First published 2004
by Routledge
2 Park Square, Milton Park, Abingdon, Oxon, OX14 4RN

Simultaneously published in the USA and Canada
by Routledge
270 Madison Ave, New York NY 10016

Routledge is an imprint of the Taylor & Francis Group

Transferred to Digital Printing 2007

© 2004 Gill Dixon and Lois M. Addy

Typeset in Palatino by
Keystroke, Jacaranda Lodge, Wolverhampton

British Library Cataloguing in Publication Data
A catalogue record for this book is available from the British Library

Library of Congress Cataloging in Publication Data
Dixon, Gill, 1960–
 Making inclusion work for children with dyspraxia : practical
 strategies for teachers / Gill Dixon and Lois M. Addy.
  p. cm.
 Includes bibliographical references and index.
 1. Inclusive education. 2. Apraxia. I. Addy, Lois M. (Lois
 Margaret), 1960– II. Title.
 LC1200.D59 2004
 371.9′046–dc22   2003020101

ISBN 0–415–31489–5

Contents

Figures

Preface

When we first mentioned to a colleague that we were involved in writing a book on the subject of dyspraxia, her response was 'Not another book on dyspraxia . . . what are you going to write that hasn't been written before?'. Indeed there are numerous books on the market aiming to help readers to understand the issues surrounding dyspraxia, which range from how to gain an accurate diagnosis, the cerebral function in a person with dyspraxia, characteristics of a child with dyspraxia, potential 'cures' for dyspraxia, through to a range of intervention strategies which can 'help' the individual, cope at home, at school and at play. So what has this book got to offer which is potentially different to others?

First, both authors share a passionate concern that the reader gains an insight into exactly what it is like to 'suffer' from what is often termed the 'hidden handicap' owing to its subtle but profound manifestations. To gain an impression, from the inside-out, of the trials and tribulations, the achievements and failures, the confusions and frustrations of living with dyspraxia from the child's perspective and as such the voice of the child will echo throughout the chapters ahead. If we simply succeed in helping you, the reader, to understand dyspraxia from the child's perspective, and to see the world as he does, we know that we will have helped children with dyspraxia to be met with empathy and compassion, the consequence of which will be tolerance and consideration, the first step towards educational and social inclusion. Children with dyspraxia have to struggle with many seemingly simple activities of daily life and strive to be accepted and integrated within their peer group at home and at school. Their lives can be likened to salmon that have to put in an enormous effort in order to swim upstream against the fast flowing current to simply survive within a society where tolerance towards poor physical prowess is lacking.

Second, we would like readers to see that although there are a range of characteristics and modes of presentation which are typical to many children with dyspraxia we want to stress the individuality of each child. We wish to emphasise that each child is a unique individual and as such has a preferred way of coping with his difficulties, some of which may be more acceptable and successful than others. We want you to realise that similarities in characteristics do not automatically give rise to children adopting similar learning styles, and that prescription intervention will not necessarily work to improve the child's functional skills. To reiterate our intention we want you to 'appreciate the cake rather than focus on the ingredients'.

Third, both authors are determined to help those meeting children with dyspraxia, be they teachers, learning support assistants, scout masters, neighbours or friends to understand their special way of viewing their world, to accept this and to strive for ways to *include* fully the individual in a positive and accepting manner thus promoting both social and educational inclusion. The alternative title to this book would be 'From Confusion to Inclusion'. This emphasises our concern that once you have first understood the child and second, gained an impression of the treatment interventions available, that you can then, in collaboration with the child, work out the best approaches which can maximise the child's potential. This will involve the creative use of resources, and flexibility in teaching approaches, which occasionally may be controversial. The results of this approach will show how these children can succeed and make a positive contribution to their class, school and society as a whole.

Fourth, we hope to provide a number of practical strategies to help the readers have a repertoire of ideas to discuss with each child and together to address the collection of needs which are impacting on each child's functional skills. These will address the key occupations with which children with dyspraxia struggle, for example literacy, physical education, and social development.

Finally, the unique positions of the authors serve to bring a wealth of experience and numerous examples to this publication. All the examples are taken directly from individuals who have been met by the authors in the context of professional or personal experience.

Gill Dixon is a mother of a 13-year-old child who has complex needs including dyspraxia. She writes from the viewpoint of how her son's condition has impacted on his development (emotionally, socially and physically), the life of his brother, her life, her family and marriage. She can avidly express the moments where she has shed tears of joy, and those of sadness as her son has faced the struggles of school, peer relationships, activities of daily living, alongside the physiological changes of puberty, and societal acceptance in a culture where individuality is treated with caution.

Gill is also a Consultant and Independent Adviser for parents and professionals. In this role she teaches extensively to various groups sharing her concern that children with dyspraxia are understood and accepted. As an adviser she has run a helpline from her home for many years, offering advice and support to many parents and children, at all hours of the day and night. She has a repertoire of examples of real incidences where children have been misunderstood and as such abused so that their confidence has been deeply scarred.

Lois Addy also writes from a dual perspective as a practising occupational therapist. Lois has worked in the field of paediatrics for over twenty years working with children with a range of special needs but predominantly children with dyspraxia in both hospital-based clinics, special and mainstream schools, the child's home, and a variety of community settings. As a therapist, she has worked within a multidisciplinary team alongside physiotherapy and speech therapy colleagues, and understands the frustrations experienced by parents as they wait for the child to receive help from the finite resources available. Through this role as a clinician Lois is able to give examples of individual children who have received differing forms of therapeutic intervention and share the successes and failures of her own clinical practice.

As a senior lecturer, Lois has been able to teach both nationally and internationally on a variety of subjects relating to dyspraxia, and has had the opportunity to research a variety of aspects of the condition, namely: handwriting development, perception and maths, aspects of physical education, social skills and self-esteem, and unlocking motivation through identifying learning styles. Through her experiences Lois can provide many evidence-based practical strategies which have been suggested by professionals, parents and children with whom she has come into contact.

The diversity and richness of experience of the two authors, means that we can look at this condition and the children it affects in a truly holistic way with actual examples of good practice, theoretical knowledge, hands-on strategies and a real empathy for these individuals. Together we sought to write a book which would both challenge readers to invest their time and energy into understanding how they can best address the needs of the individual with dyspraxia. In order to do this we have divided the book into two Parts.

Part I aims to help you to truly understand dyspraxia. It will initially attempt to define and describe the term dyspraxia, while reducing the confusion, which surrounds today's terminology. It will describe developmental differences and typical characteristics, while simultaneously reiterating the importance of individuality. It will place these symptoms in the context of their impact on occupational performance, both at home, at school and at play.

Within Part II we will provide practical solutions to a range of activities which are problematic for children with dyspraxia, such as: literacy, including handwriting, the impact of perceptuo-motor dysfunction on mathematics, inclusive physical education, developing social skills while raising self-esteem and self-confidence, and general strategies to adopt in the classroom and at home.

This part will also serve to provide some useful strategies to help to address each child's special needs. It will initially provide an overview of treatment or intervention approaches and when and why certain approaches are adopted.

Throughout the text we will demonstrate the impact of combining understanding with remedial strategies in reducing stress on the family, the teacher and most importantly, the child. We will culminate in challenging your personal perception of social inclusion, which will help you to face up to your fears surrounding special education issues. We will finally lead you to further sources of advice, useful information, and provide references as to the evidence-base, which supports this text.

To summarise, this book is not about curing or self-congratulating, nor is it simply a manual of easily referenced do's and don'ts. It is a book about real understanding, empathy and acknowledgement, about working together and about acknowledging the difficulties that individuals with dyspraxia face and about working with them in an effort to make their experience in mainstream school, at home, and with friends as positive and successful as it can be.

We do not profess to have all the answers but we ask that you read our book and that you

- *Consider* where you are, how you feel, and what has influenced you.
- *Reflect* on your practice and your experiences.
- *Challenge* yourself to say hand on heart that the notion of inclusion doesn't involve you. Whatever your personal beliefs on inclusion, you must question whether you are promoting full integration through your current practice, attitudes and adaptability.

- *Accept* that children with a variety of special educational needs including dyspraxia *will* access the mainstream curriculum whether you believe in inclusion or not and knowing this question, how you can integrate these children fully.
- *Change*. By asking yourself how you can, and gathering the knowledge and expertise to do so.
- *Include*. To make your attitude one of wanting to include people with dyspraxia for what they are, and not because you feel you can 'improve', 'alter' or cure them.

We hope you enjoy the book and that it leaves you with the knowledge that you really can make a difference.

Please note

As more boys than girls are diagnosed with dyspraxia we have chosen to use the term 'he' and 'his' throughout the text, which we feel will allow for easier reading. We have also tended to use 'Mother' when talking about the child's carer as it is often (but not always) the mother who is primarily involved. This is not meant as any disrespect to fathers or other significant people. The reader will also notice that at times the authors use the terms 'special need' and 'disability' seemingly interchangeably. In truth we would like to dispense with the term 'special needs' altogether as this categorises children and in some way sets them apart. It would be more appropriate to say that these children have 'barriers to learning and participation' (Booth and Ainscow, 2002). We do not wish to get into the politics of definition but as we are interested in inclusive practice we believe that while terminology is important in the 'inclusion arena' we recognise that people choose to at times call dyspraxia, a special need, a disability, a handicap or a difference. The terminology used can depend on the environment, profession or particular leaning of the person using the term and for the purposes of this book that is not important.

Acknowledgements

Thanks are due to the following people for their contributions: Gemma for her drawings, Emma Illingworth for her willingness to help, Keith Holland, Lucky Duck Publishing Ltd, LDA Ltd and Magination press for allowing us to reproduce useful samples of their work, and all of you who contributed your stories and experiences. You know who you are.

Special thanks are due to our families: Phil and Geoff for their understanding and patience as we enthused about this subject. Bethany and Charlotte for sleeping while Mummy wrote and to Joe and Max who taught us so much. You are all wonderful.

Introduction

The inclusion of children with special educational needs (SEN) into mainstream schools has been one of the most positive steps in social and educational policy for decades. Inclusion can be defined as 'a shared vision which is one of developing relationships and a curriculum that ensures that everyone feels valued, respected and reaches a high level of achievement' (Ainscow, 1996, p. 15). By allowing a child to attend a school near to his home he has the opportunity to integrate with his peers and break down segregated barriers associated with special education establishments. This has allowed children with a range of difficulties to participate in the National Curriculum, which may be modified or adapted according to individual requirements.

Prior to this initiative, children with SEN were educated in schools specifically geared for children with 'moderate or severe learning difficulty, or those accommodating children with physical disabilities. These schools did provide a rich environment with small class sizes, and a high ratio of experienced staff, along with specialised resources such as hydrotherapy pools. However, attendance at these schools often involved children travelling some distance from their home to attend. Therefore they were unable to learn with their neighbours and friends, and often undertook a restricted curriculum. Socially such children frequently became labelled by their disability, stigmatised by their 'difference' and restricted in social interaction. Inclusion recommended that students with SEN should be placed in age-appropriate general education classrooms in neighbourhood schools.

The consequence of inclusion is that within the majority of schools in the UK, children now attend who have a vast array of difficulties be these physical, emotional, cognitive or sensory. Unlike the previous segregated system, teachers now have the complicated task of having to address the educational needs of these children with limited resources and information.

One of the most positive occurrences which have happened as inclusion has gained momentum is an increased awareness by many teachers and related professionals that many underachieving children already receiving mainstream education, who had previously been labelled awkward, hyperactive, clumsy, difficult and problem-learners, actually had a specific learning difficulty. These difficulties did not warrant disciplinary management, but understanding and specialist help. Consequently there is now an escalated awareness of children with conditions such as Attention Deficit (hyperactivity) Disorder (ADHD), dyslexia and Autistic Spectrum Disorders (ASD). This was also particularly true of children with dyspraxia whose verbal comprehension (and often expression) did not match up with their physical presentation and educational productivity.

One of the main concerns now is that teachers need to grasp the individual needs of children with a vast array of difficulties. If a child has entered school with a diagnosis it is slightly easier to get information which would help accommodate the child's needs. However, many of the symptoms of dyspraxia are not recognised until the child is at least 5 years old, and it's only when specific tasks are required of the child in year one at school that their difficulties become evident. Without help the teacher then has to decide whether the child is simply a slow developer, immature or whether there is a specific reason/cause for his difficulties. These early years are crucial to the child as misunderstanding the signals can have serious effects on the quality of interaction, which in turn can affect the child's self-confidence and self-esteem. This can signal the child's attitude to his future educational experiences.

It is not the fault of the teacher, who has to address the individual requirements of up to thirty-five children, but it demonstrates the need for education through instruction, specialist consultation and literature such as this publication.

Consider the following, somewhat extreme but true example.

An 8-year-old boy who was known to have dyspraxia wanted to use the toilet during a school playtime. He knew he was very slow to dress and undress, he felt very insecure with his feet dangling down from the toilet, and he had real difficulties in cleansing himself when he had finished. He faced a degree of teasing all the time he was at school but couldn't face it at a time when he craved complete privacy and needed additional time. He dealt with this by continually retreating to the back of the queue hoping eventually that he would be the only one left in the toilets. The bell sounded for the end of playtime and the boy left the toilet in an agitated manner because he knew that although his need was desperate he wasn't able to use the toilet on this occasion. Frightened of being told off again for 'being last' and 'holding the class up' he returned to class. Half-way through the lesson he knew he could not wait until the lesson ended and he summoned up the courage to ask if he might use the toilet. The teacher reminded him that pupils were meant to use break times for toileting purposes and asked him to attend to his work for the moment. He became increasingly desperate and found the courage to ask again. His peers giggled, the teacher sighed and once again he was denied permission. He was now totally unable to concentrate and noticeably fidgeted and interrupted the class. The teacher reflected that he was becoming a 'behavioural problem'. On the third time of asking the teacher's temper was becoming a little frayed, the class a little restless, the boy increasingly desperate, but the teacher would not employ any degree of flexibility in her interpretation of the class rules. To the teacher's horror, the boy defecated in his pants. His distress was intense and school became for him a psychological nightmare from that day forth as he faced constant teasing and reminders of the day he soiled his pants.

This was a very real occurrence in a mainstream school and it is, along with other stories, the motivation behind this book. We hope that by the time you have finished reading the book you will understand why these stories are still in evidence and how they can be avoided. It is easy to read this story in disbelief and assume that we would never behave as this teacher did but there is a possibility that we might, or that we already have done. Of course it is an extreme example, but nonetheless an actual one. We will revisit this boy at the end of the book and hopefully feel able to understand why this happened and why it would be inappropriate to apportion blame. The situation might have been handled differently if the teacher had better understood what made this little lad behave as he did.

This example can give you some impression of how difficult it is for a teacher of a large class to read the subtle signals and compensatory behaviour adopted by the child to protect himself from ridicule. It also shows you why teachers sometimes appear to be defensive to parents and why parents sometimes appear to be aggressive towards professionals. More than anything it demonstrates the need to understand the condition 'dyspraxia' in its entirety. This in itself will result in empathy and acceptance, even before tactics are introduced to help with specific needs.

Therefore the first part of this book will look at the contentious issue of what dyspraxia/DCD (developmental coordination disorder) is and isn't. Referring to available research it asks why some people are dyspraxic and who should diagnose this complex and subtle disability? It will discuss the characteristics and the affects of the condition on living and learning.

Part I

Understanding dyspraxia

Chapter 1

Dyspraxia/DCD:

Definitions, aetiology and incidence

Dyspraxia is certainly not a new condition and research is abundant if the investigator is aware of the various synonyms used to describe the same condition. Dupre made reference to it as early as 1911 (Hulme and Lord, 1986) and McKinlay and Gordon (1989) make reference to 365 articles pertaining to dyspraxia and its effects. Portwood (2002) points us to 42 articles relating to dyspraxia, which have been published in the last two years. Clumsy child syndrome, minimal brain dysfunction, *l'enfant maladroit*, motor learning difficulty, developmental apraxia and agnosia, sensory integrative dysfunction and more recently developmental coordination disorder (DCD) are all names used to describe the same condition.

Developmental dyspraxia or Developmental Coordination disorder (DCD), as it is more recently referred to, is a condition in which interest and research has escalated in recent years. With the emphasis on inclusion in our mainstream schools there is a growing awareness of the fact that teachers really are meeting children with dyspraxia in their classrooms and that there really is a need to be able to support and guide them appropriately and successfully.

Defining dyspraxia is not as easy as it sounds because there are a number of definitions in circulation. While these do not really conflict with each other, they do give rise to a great deal of confusion. To add to this confusion, parents are often frustrated by the fact that they are told that their children have 'dyspraxic tendencies' or have 'some features' rather than that they are dyspraxic.

It is easy to say what dyspraxia is *not*. It is not a child treading on other people's toes on purpose. It is not a child who is intentionally slow at dressing after PE; it is not naughtiness or disobedience. Yet, all too often this is what it is perceived to be. This misconception of what dyspraxia is and the impact it has may leave a child disillusioned and disaffected until eventually the child needlessly becomes a 'behavioural difficulty' or is described as 'challenging'. In truth the challenge is not the child's but a challenge to the systems through which that child passes, which so often do not serve him well. Non recognition of dyspraxia, or worse a tendency to believe that it does not really exist is a crime against the child, his family and ultimately society.

Unlike dyslexia, dyspraxia is poorly acknowledged, and yet as a condition it may well hinder and inhibit a child's educational and social progress since it involves all those aspects of functioning which we describe as relating to 'doing' (Dyspraxia Foundation).

Definitions

The numbers of definitions in circulation relating to dyspraxia do not all incorporate exactly the same features. The Dyspraxia Foundation, a charitable support organisation for children and adults defined dyspraxia in its *Dyspraxia Explained* leaflet as:

> An impairment or immaturity of the organisation of movement and in many individuals there may be associated problems of language, perception and thought.
>
> (1987)

This is a comprehensive definition in that it highlights the child's difficulty with motor coordination, but it does not highlight that it is the *organisation* of perception, thought and sometimes language, which is affected in those with dyspraxia. Nor does it refer to the fact that the majority of children with dyspraxia have 'normal' intelligence. This emphasises the fact that many of the specific learning difficulties experienced by children with dyspraxia are *not* due to cognitive delay per se, but specific problems in organising and processing incoming information.

The actual word dyspraxia comes from the Greek word 'dys' which means difficulty or ill and 'praxia' meaning 'doing, acting, deed and practice'. Therefore dyspraxia literally means 'difficulties in doing' or 'ill doing'. This is very accurate in that it highlights the child's inability to act promptly, or to initiate immediately a response, to information received from the environment, be this in the form of verbal instruction, demonstration or interpretation of sensory stimuli. After all, 'doing' or 'praxis' requires conscious thought and needs the brain to conceptualise, organise and direct purposeful interaction with the physical world (Ayres *et al.*, 1987).

Further definitions refer to observing marked motor organisational difficulties in the absence of neurological symptoms. This is important as many childhood conditions where motor coordination is dysfunctional have a neurological basis, i.e. cerebral palsy, tuberous sclerosis. Poustie *et al.* (1997) for example states that

> [Dyspraxia] is a specific learning difficulty in gross and fine motor planning which is not caused by muscle/nerve damage.
>
> (p. 57)

And Penso (1999) refers to

> Difficulty in planning and organising movements at a cerebral level.
>
> (p. 86)

Even though there is an absence of overt neurological signs, based on conventional medical tests, in children with dyspraxia, there is increased evidence that children with dyspraxia exhibit 'soft' neurological signs (Denckla, 1984; McPhillips *et al.*, 2000). These present as residual primitive reflex patterns and can often be seen when a child is active, running, jumping and undertaking fine-motor activities.

The term developmental coordination disorder (DCD) has been used more recently and is often used interchangeably (and incorrectly) with the term dyspraxia. The American Psychiatric Association (APA), coined this term in 1987 to describe the child with:

> Marked impairment in the development of motor co-ordination that is not explainable by mental retardation and that is not due to a physical disorder. The diagnosis is only made if this impairment significantly interferes with academic achievement or with activities of daily living.
>
> (APA, 1994, p. 53)

This infers that performance in daily living activities such as class work, play, and self-care tasks, that require motor coordination is substantially below that expected, given the person's chronological age and measured intelligence. Developmental dyspraxia is a subtype of DCD and is recognised by a marked impairment in gross and fine-motor *organisation* (which may or may not influence articulation and speech) which are influenced by poor perceptual regulation. These difficulties present as an inability to *plan and organise purposeful movement*. Therefore children with dyspraxia know how to undertake activities but cannot organise the movements to achieve them. These difficulties do not have an overt neurological or genetic origin, and are not explicable by developmental delay. Individuals have normal intellect, but the effects of the perceptual–motor disorganisation results in an inability to perform many daily living activities.

Incidence

Recent studies suggest that between 5 and 18 per cent of individuals in the United Kingdom are affected by dyspraxia (Godfrey, 1994; Hall, 1994; Marks, 1994; Portwood, 1996). To put this into context; there is likely to be at least one child with dyspraxia in every typical class of twenty-five children! Its consequences are complex and far-reaching, affecting the child's social, motor, language and perceptual skills and reasoning ability. Current research shows that dyspraxia affects far more boys than it does girls. Some may suggest that the number of girls affected may be clouded by the fact that they have a tendency towards withdrawal and shyness in the classroom and so do not draw attention to themselves as much as boys have a tendency to do, by being noisy, disruptive or difficult.

What causes dyspraxia?

The cause is far from clear although there are a number of theories to date. Madeleine Portwood (1996, p. 8) writes

> There is evidence to suggest that in the case of the child with dyspraxia the reinforced interconnections between the nerve cells in the cerebral cortex are reduced in number. The cortex persists in a state of immaturity, which varies greatly between individuals.

This increases the idea that premature delivery is a key factor in dyspraxia. The failure of the neurones in the brain to form adequate connections causes a slowing in the brain's ability to process information. This can also result in an inability to integrate different sensory information to enhance the development of body schema for motor planning, i.e. sensory integration (Brooks-Gunn *et al.*, 1992; Padsman *et al.*, 1998). Difficulties during the pre and perinatal period, infection and alcohol/substance abuse have also been linked to potential causes of dyspraxia. An increasing concern is multiple births. This has become more significant with the use of *in vitro* fertilisation (IVF) and the later age of parenting.

All these theories read well and are interesting, but none are proven and it is safer to pay regard to Henderson, Dubowitz and Jongmans who in 1994 stated that:

> There are many things about dyspraxia we do not yet understand . . . We know already that there must be more than one cause but we are far from being able to provide a list.
>
> (*Midline*, November p. 2)

Can it be cured?

There is no known cure at the present time, but that does not mean that children with dyspraxia will necessarily mature into dysfunctional adults, far from it. Individuals with dyspraxia are valuable members of society who can have a bright future if their difficulties are acknowledged and addressed.

Do children grow out of it?

In general, children do not 'grow out' of dyspraxia. Children do learn to accommodate their difficulties and there is evidence that early intervention can have beneficial results (Losse *et al.*, 1991). Children who do not receive help suffer low self-esteem and self-confidence. They are likely to develop behavioural and emotional difficulties, and *do not* reach their academic potential.

Diagnosis

Not knowing a definitive cause can make the selection of correct diagnosis and treatment difficult, and at grass roots level parents and teachers can be left awash in a sea of confusion. Such uncertainty often leads to disbelief, anger and exasperation for parents and teachers who are trying to meet the needs of these children who seemingly need a label if they are to attract any resources. It would appear that the more that is understood about dyspraxia, the more confusion arises. Kirby (1999) sensibly suggests that 'there is a need for clarification and standardisation so that we all use the same language'.

There is no doubt that there are some diagnosticians who have a great deal more interest, expertise and experience of dyspraxia than others do. So a doctor may suggest that a child has 'dyspraxic tendencies' rather than having dyspraxia, because they are not confident enough to diagnose it or because the child they are seeing does not truly fit into the diagnostic criteria. Or it may be that the child displays other symptoms, which have a leaning towards a different condition. It is not that the diagnostician is being indecisive or difficult, but more that they are giving a 'diagnosis' to the best of their ability and belief. It may be that they feel a further period of monitoring is needed, or they may truly believe that the child has a developmental delay rather than true dyspraxia, and so they do not want to label the child in haste and possibly inappropriately. Rarely do children fall into neat diagnostic categories. Therefore patience and trust is required to allow those in a position to determine dyspraxia, to do so.

Parents do need to be aware of the reasons for the delay in obtaining a diagnosis if they are to make sense of what is happening to them and their families. An example of this can be given by suggesting that if the same child was presented to three different professionals for a diagnosis they may leave the surgery of each with a different diagnosis. That does not mean that one is right and two are wrong, but these professionals may have used different standardised tests to diagnose the child, and they may have a great deal of experience and interest in dyspraxia or very little. It is fair to say that if many parents and teachers were given a list of features that relate to dyslexia, dyspraxia and Asperger's syndrome in a pre-school aged child they may have huge difficulties in ascribing a condition to a child. The features can be confusingly similar. The diagnostician then should not only contribute a diagnosis or label (or lack of one) but they should explain exactly what they mean by that term at the time of assessment and diagnosis. This would furnish families and teachers with a framework from which they can work and gain further understanding.

This leads onto the dangers of a diagnosis being made by someone who is not really in a position to give one, for example a teacher, a parent or a health visitor. It may be that they are perfectly correct in highlighting features of a child's performance that require observation and investigation but this is not diagnosis. In order for the complexities of the condition to be discovered and assessed a range of assessment criteria may be used. A psychologist may use a number of psychological tests to arrive at a diagnosis, which will highlight areas of difficulty but those assessments will not necessarily look at the visual perceptual difficulties or any speech, language and communication difficulties that the child may be experiencing. A speech and language therapist may give a very detailed report relating to verbal dyspraxia, but this does not establish motor, or perceptual difficulties. Therefore, in an ideal world, a team of people who can feed in their particular expertise to build up a clear picture of the whole child and not fragment him into parts and features, and ultimately objectify him will make a diagnosis. However, reality is often very different from the ideal, and many parents and teachers discover barriers to their understanding, confusion in the terminology used and huge difficulties in getting definitive diagnosis and intervention. The road to diagnosis can be a very bumpy one indeed.

At least as important as all the definitions, terminology and research is the fact that dyspraxia is part of a person. It is an important part, not to be despised, neglected, cured or denied. From the debates surrounding definition and diagnosis, it can be seen that people with dyspraxia do not form a neat, homogeneous group, who can follow a course of treatment and all become 'better' people for it. Dyspraxia is a process, an experience, and a life. If a child has asthma, those people concerned with his or her care do not deny its existence. They try to understand what it means for them, and how they might alleviate symptoms or prevent attacks. It is part of that child and the experience they have of life as an asthmatic is unique to them. It becomes an important part of who they are and it affects the way they are and the things they do. The majority of people respond positively to its existence, fearing the consequences of lack of knowledge, or seeing its management as important and meaningful. The same should apply to dyspraxia. It is part of what makes up a unique individual. Pretending it doesn't exist or isn't there is not useful, and potentially very harmful. Dyspraxia must be acknowledged and attempts made to try to understand what it means for the child. How it is managed should be important, and teachers and parents should be fearful of the consequences of bad management, just as they would be for the asthmatic. Teachers and parents have the ability and responsibility to help to mould a valuable and unique member of an inclusive society. They also have the potential to strip the very soul from children, by removing their confidence, denting their self-esteem and denying a very important part of who they are.

Dyspraxia is not new and recognition of it is increasing. In an effort to alleviate stress from teachers, parents and the individuals themselves, all those concerned with the development of children have a duty to try to familiarise themselves with its effects, to understand its impact, and appreciate that they can be part of a child's success or failure.

Chapter 2

Developmental differences

> You will have seen him: seven years old, shirt half out of his trousers, one sock up, one sock down, shoes on the wrong feet, shoe laces invariably trailing. His pencil will be chewed and broken, books dog-eared, backs torn off. He appears to be always interfering with the other children. He is the last one ready both before and after PE, and his movement and dance have to be seen to be believed! You will have heard him . . . this child who always calls out in class, who always has the last word, and invariably interrupts. You will have felt him, probably standing on your toes to get near enough to talk to you! In the process of reaching you he will have tipped at least one child off his chair, knocked a book or painting to the floor, nudged someone's elbow, etc . . . He is often described as simply 'odd', but he may appear aggressive, lazy, stubborn or careless.
>
> (Parkin and Padley, 1986, p. 1)

This quote was written as a description of a child with dyspraxia. It is serious in its intentions, but creates a rather comical picture of an individual who endures a complex, and poorly understood condition. There is a tendency for people to declare their understanding of children with dyspraxia as people who are clumsy, and poorly coordinated. There seems to be little awareness of the subtle underlying processes which cause such disturbances. It is indeed a very complex condition which affects the whole child in almost every aspect of living and learning. It is therefore important to provide an overview of motor, perceptual and oral-motor differences and difficulties experienced by the child with dyspraxia to give a better understanding of what a child with dyspraxia has to contend with every day of the week.

The child with dyspraxia often appears awkward and accident-prone. He always seems to be the child who disrupts the dinner queue or manages to trip over a snail that is meandering across the football field! Parents often report that 'they fall over fresh air'. This is the child who as he grows older becomes irritating as he repeatedly invades other people's space, treads on toes, asks endless questions or knocks things over in the science lab. It is the child who appears 'black and blue' from all the bumps and trips they appear to have. We have a responsibility to find out why this is the case, why do children with dyspraxia appear so poorly co-ordinated, why are they unable to manoeuvre around objects, and how are they perceiving their environment? We also need to consider that a proportion of children have verbal dyspraxia. To answer these questions we need to consider three key aspects of dyspraxia: gross/fine-motor coordination, perception and oral-motor coordination.

Gross/fine-motor coordination

Almost every activity performed in life requires the initiation of a motor response and involves motor control. Even seemingly stationary activities such as watching the TV requires the occasional shift in position to maintain comfort and improve circulation. Sedentary occupations such as reading also require visual scanning and the ability to cross the midline of the body to turn a page over. Most tasks require some form of planned movement, and the more complex the task, the more covert energy is utilised to plan a strategy for success.

To achieve even the simplest task, a sequential assessment of the environment is required prior to formulating a motor strategy to achieve the end result. In order to develop motor control one must firstly *understand* the goal, *formulate* a plan and then *execute* the plan in order to succeed. This seemingly simple achievement is dependent upon interpreting correctly incoming sensory information from the environment in an intact and efficient manner.

Therefore in order to simply reach for, and grasp a ball, information is required as to the size, potential weight and surface texture of the ball. Detail is also required as to how far the body is away from the ball, and how much the arm must stretch before the ball can be grasped. Intact hand–eye coordination is required to position the hand on the ball and pressure sense is required to grasp the fingers around the ball. Judgement is also required as to how much the body must lean forward to enable grasp of the ball, while maintaining the body's stability against gravity. Such complex actions for such a seemingly simple task! With experience and practice this simple act becomes unconscious and the motor plan formulated automatic in neuro-typical children. Unfortunately this is not the case for children with dyspraxia.

We know that children with dyspraxia do not receive the same messages regarding incoming sensory information as do other children, this is possibly due to inadequate connections within the brain, and therefore their response to information is distorted. It is therefore important to attempt to understand the various systems which enable us to undertake fine and gross motor activities; it is not simply a case of weak muscles or 'floppy limbs'. Children with dyspraxia do have the same skeletal muscles and movement opportunities as other children, what differs is how the additional information required, which helps us to develop refined, precise movement, is processed.

There are three key systems which are responsible for providing information which will help us to develop controlled movement, each of equal importance to the other. First, we have a refined *sensory system*, which includes touch, sight, taste, hearing and smell. Each of these senses operates through complex electromagnetic or electrochemical impulses, which generate messages to the brain and are in turn interpreted according to experiences past and present. Initially a child is dependent upon sight and touch to interpret objects, shapes and people in his world. Taste and smell add a further dimension. Touch is a particularly useful sense in respect to motor control as early exploration of a toy requires a young child to experience and experiment with pressure through the fingers to hold a toy. Too little and the toy falls and is lost, too much and the toy may lose its movement qualities.

A second system, the *proprioceptive system*, provides information about where your limbs are in relation to your body, without the need for sight. Located within our joints and muscles there are special receptors that monitor muscle stretch, and identify the exact position of each limb. It is because of our proprioceptive system that we are able to undertake fine and gross motor tasks without the need to look at what our arms/hands and legs/feet are doing. It is due to this arrangement that we can, for example; tie an apron round our waist, comb the back of our hair, undo a bra strap or wipe ourselves after going to the toilet. For each of these activities we rely on touch and proprioception to inform us where to move our arms and hands. It is also because of these receptors that we learn how to place objects down precisely on a given surface. Proprioceptors are responsible for the careful, slow control required in many activities.

Unfortunately, inadequate proprioception is experienced by many if not the majority of individuals with dyspraxia. The information received by the proprioceptors is either not as acute, or 'dampened' in the child with dyspraxia. Consequently they do not receive the correct information as to where their limbs are in relation to the body. This interferes with refined control, grasp, release and coordinated movement. When a glass is placed on a table, the child with proprioceptive deficits cannot monitor the position of the arm and will either slam the glass down or misplace where the surface is, this is why they are often called 'ham-fisted' or 'clumsy'. Similarly gross motor activities are not refined and the child with dyspraxia often appears ungainly, heavy-footed and awkward.

The inability to understand accurate limb position can also affect activities where the hands cannot be seen, so wiping the bottom after toileting may be problematic, which in turn can affect personal hygiene. Dressing will be poor as clothes out of sight may remain dishevelled. Hair may be unkempt due to the inability to comb what cannot be seen. In respect to gross motor activities, motor control may be poor and there may be an over-reliance on vision to compensate. Therefore the child can only ride a bike if observing the movements of his feet on the pedals rather than concentrating on control and direction.

A third system at play in the development of motor control and movement is the *vestibular system*. Located within our inner ears we have tiny hairs, which waver as we move the position of our head, these movements send electrochemical impulses to the brain to assess movement and position on the head in relation to the body. It is because of these receptors that we are able to maintain our head up-right against gravity, and that we can judge movement forward, backward and sideways, we can also control rotation movements. This system helps us to control the speed of a movement. So, to refer to the previous example of reaching for a ball, by leaning forward, the tiny hair like receptors will waver and send signals that the head is moving forward and monitor and adapt to the velocity of that movement.

Again this system can be affected in children with dyspraxia causing them to lack control in the speed of their movements. This is why the words 'careful' and 'look out' are frequently muted to these children whose movements appear out of control. To really understand what it is like for the child to experience this consider a time when you have encountered an ear ache or ear infection. On these occasions the first thing that is affected is balance, immediately we start to feel unsure of our movements, begin to feel giddy and sometimes even nauseous. This is how certain children with dyspraxia feel on a regular basis.

We can now see how the sensory system, proprioceptive system and vestibular system help us to control and refine movements, and that difficulties in these areas will give rise to serious consequences in the development of motor coordination.

It also explains why a child with dyspraxia does things in a hesitant, inefficient way and is often accident-prone. Their posture and balance are often poor and they appear weak. They display difficulties with complicated activities (such as dressing and riding a bicycle). They may have particular difficulties with fine-motor activities, such as jigsaws, drawing and using a ruler to draw a line, but they do become masters of avoidance at a very early age.

Mary recounts:

The fact that Danny never tried building blocks, or preferred not to do the jigsaws, and always chose the ride on toys that he could push along with his feet rather than pedal, had never been an issue with me. Then I realised that it wasn't a preference on his part, but avoidance. He really couldn't do these things because they were just too difficult for him. He was always into the touchy, feely things, dough to play with, sand and paint. I just thought he liked those things. I had never observed what he avoided and that he cleverly and sensibly had strategies in place at a very early age, which wouldn't draw attention to his difficulties.

Gill recalled:

I can remember when my son was little and got really muddy in the garden. I decided to sluice him down in the utility room sink before taking him upstairs for a bath. I stood him in the sink and asked him to sit down on the draining board. He just didn't know how to do it. He had sat down automatically on thousands of occasions, but he had never been asked to sit on a draining board before. I had to teach him all over again! That really brought the effect of dyspraxia home to me.

These examples give a clear impression of the almost bewildering qualities of the child with dyspraxia. They also demonstrate how the child subtly uses his intellect to avoid and manipulate his environment in order to give the impression of 'normality'. It is only when we can comprehend the development of motor skills and learn how this differs in a child with dyspraxia that we can begin to empathise with the struggles faced during even simple motor tasks.

We have seen how dysfunctional proprioception (remember that system that allows us to know where our limbs are in relation to our body without the need for sight), vestibular and sensory systems influence motor coordination. What we also need to address is how these systems impact on the child's perceptual maturation. We also need to appreciate the effects of dysfunctional visual and auditory perception on the child's fine-motor and gross motor control, and learning ability. Perception and motor control progress together simultaneously from an early age; each influencing the other. It is very interesting to observe a child making sense of his environment through visual and auditory perceptual processes. It is possible to see how dysfunctional perception experienced by children with dyspraxia, has a bearing on their understanding of their environment and subsequent learning. Therefore the next section of this chapter will look at the subtle impact of perception on refining motor control and cognition.

Perceptual–motor development

In the previous section, the importance of our sensory system was highlighted, along with proprioception, which helps us to judge body position, and our vestibular system, which helps us to judge movement, speed and balance. It is now important to explain how these systems influence visual and, auditory perception. To do so we need to state first what we mean by perception.

Perception is how we *interpret* the world through our five different senses. It arises through an awareness of elements in the environment which we experience through sight, smell, taste, touch and sound. It requires a conscious, cognitive interpretation of incoming information, which is often based on previous experiences. Perception requires an individual to develop a mental image of an object and necessitates a sense of consciousness. Visual perception is how we interpret what we see. This differs from vision, which is the special sense by which the qualities of an object, such as colour, luminosity, shape and size are seen and defined by the eye.

To explain this further we have divided the various aspects into different sections; this may be viewed as a purist way of addressing perception as in reality many areas of perception overlap or are intertwined. However, it is a useful way of considering the various aspects, which make up perceptual discernment. It can also help to explain why certain tasks prove problematic for children with dyspraxia and can be a starting point from which to address and remediate functional difficulties. We will start with the most basic aspect of perception, which is hand–eye coordination.

Hand–eye coordination

Hand–eye coordination, or visual motor coordination as it is often termed, is the ability to coordinate a hand movement to a visual goal. Whenever we reach for an object our vision guides our hand to the goal. This is one of the earliest levels of perceptual development acquired during early infancy. In order to reach a toy we need vision to see the object and muscle response to extend our arm forward to reach for the toy. We also need to initiate this response so need a sense of curiosity, interest and desire to investigate and explore our surroundings. This desire to learn from our environment demonstrates our intellect or cognitive ambition. Children who have severe learning difficulties often lack this initiative and therefore limit the learning that can be achieved from exploring the environment.

Once an object has been grasped it is explored through touch and its properties are experienced. Often in young children a toy is mouthed, this occurs as the child differentiates between objects, which are for sustenance, such as food and those with interesting surface properties. The touch receptors around the mouth are the most sensitive of all the surface receptors. Physical exploration through touch, vision, sound (if the toy has any auditory properties) and the information gathered regarding velocity experienced through the toys weight, enables the child to develop a sense of object recognition and 'form constancy'. Dysfunctional hand–eye co-ordination occurs when proprioception, vestibular feedback and sensation of touch are not as acute as they should be. The proprioceptive system provides incorrect information as to the location of the arm and hand, and the degree of movement required in order to reach an object. In turn visual–spatial judgement is affected and precise motor control is impeded. A child who has dysfunctional hand–eye coordination will find even the simplest tasks difficult to perform. He will find dressing and undressing difficult due to the complexity of coordinating fastenings, also handwriting, cooking and baking, manual work and even the use of a knife and fork. Placement of blocks on top of one another or placing pegs in a board will also prove problematic. Placement of objects may be 'heavy' and objects easily broken. The following example demonstrates the effect of dysfunctional hand–eye coordination on the child's occupational performance.

Peter was a delightful little boy who was referred for an occupational therapy assessment at the age of 6. His teacher reported that his verbal skills were superb and that he could 'talk for England'. She also reported that he was a gifted storyteller, yet she was frustrated by his seeming inability to write stories down. She wondered whether his reluctance to write was an avoidance of written work or whether he had a genuine problem with writing. She provided an example of his handwriting, which was virtually illegible, and was very keen to have any feedback.

On our initial meeting, Peter was asked to perform some simple hand–eye coordination tasks; this included the request to make a tower with 2 cm blocks. Peter could not place more than three blocks on top of one another without them falling over, when placing the blocks he tended to place them heavily so causing the lower block to move. This simple task demonstrated that Peter experienced difficulties in proprioceptive feedback; he was unable to monitor the pressure through his upper limbs and consequently pressed down too hard. This affected hand–eye coordination to the extent that fine-motor control was severely impeded. Handwriting therefore lacked control and required considerable effort. Peter would not be able to undertake fine-motor tasks until he could learn to adjust his motor pressure more sensitively.

Peter needed to regulate proprioceptive feedback experienced particularly in his upper limbs, he was taught to do this through exercises and activities to stimulate the muscle receptors in the upper limbs while working on exercises to stabilise his shoulder girdle.

It is important, when considering hand–eye coordination that the child's vision is checked. Some children experience a condition known as hemianopia whereby an individual experiences loss of vision in one half of the visual field. This is not a characteristic of dyspraxia and usually indicates a neurological problem. Help should be sought immediately. The following non-standardised checklist can be used to give you an idea of whether a child in your care is experiencing visual or perceptual difficulties.

Confidential

Visual dysfunction checklist for Teachers

Child's name . . . . Form/Teacher Reference . . . .

I *Please circle the specific areas (if any) of difficulty the child has with reading*

VOCABULARY   WORD RECOGNITION   ORAL READING   RATE

SILENT READING   ATTENTION   INTERPRETATION   COMPREHENSION

2 Four classifications of frequency of performance traits are given:

A Meaning very often observed (many times/day)
B Meaning regularly observed (daily)
C Meaning sometimes observed
D Meaning seldom observed

Please ring the letter you best consider indicates the child's performance.

Does the child show any of the following?

a	Skipping or rereading lines or words	A	B	C	D
b	Reads too slowly	A	B	C	D
c	Use finger or marker as a pointer when reading	A	B	C	D
d	Lacks ability to remember what he has read	A	B	C	D
e	Shows fatigue or listlessness when reading	A	B	C	D
f	Complains of print 'running together' or 'jumping'	A	B	C	D
g	Gets too close to reading and writing tasks	A	B	C	D
h	Loss of attention to task at hand	A	B	C	D
i	Distracted by other activities	A	B	C	D
j	Assumes an improper or awkward sitting posture	A	B	C	D
k	Writes crookedly, poorly spaced letters, cannot stay on ruled lines, excessive pressure used	A	B	C	D
l	Orients drawing poorly on paper	A	B	C	D
m	Is seen to blink frequently	A	B	C	D
n	Rubs eyes excessively	A	B	C	D

General observations:

o	Clumsiness and difficulty manipulating own body and other objects in space available, including problems with ball control	A	B	C	D
p	Awareness of things around him in the classroom To point where he turns to look at stimulus	A	B	C	D
q	Is this child able to maintain his involvement with your instruction?	A	B	C	D

Scoring:

Any scores of '**A**', more than two scores of '**B**' and more than three or four of '**C**' suggests that prompt referral to an optometrist specialising in children's eye care is indicated.

A copy of this checklist would also be helpful to the optometrist.

(Reproduced by kind permission of: Keith Holland. Originally published by NFER as an article in *Topic* 13: spring 1995)

Visual form constancy

'Perceptual constancy is the ability to perceive an object as possessing variant properties, such as shape, position and size, in spite of the variability of the stimuli presented to the sense organs' (Frostig, 1973). As children learn to explore and experiment with new objects, they begin to develop object categories within their brain's memory bank. Initially this is basic and key features of an object are grouped together in one category or schema; for example when a child is given a ball to play with, exploration of this helps the child to create a category so that when other round objects are given, this can also fit into the same category while subtle differences are registered. A more complex example can be seen in a child's early recognition of a face. In the very young, securely attached baby, anyone who has a warm smile and who is softly spoken is viewed as 'mum', the prime care giver and source of food. It is only when the child is able to discriminate more subtle features, that he can discern the difference between mum and significant others. Face differentiation occurs at a very young age but is refined over the first year in a child's life.

Exploration and categorisation of objects enable the child to appreciate that an object viewed from another angle is in fact the same object. Consider the example below of a drinks can. Form constancy suggests that an individual seeing this can from a number of angles will still recognise it as a drinks can.

Children with dyspraxia may struggle to develop form constancy. This is due to receiving incorrect information regarding an object from a 'dampened' sense of touch. Therefore the tactile qualities of an object are not appreciated and clear categories regarding the object are not formed. A child with poor tactile reception will rely heavily on vision to make sense of new objects or those which are positioned in an unfamiliar way.

An example of this was seen when working with Isaac.

Figure 2.1 How we perceive an object from a number of angles

When Isaac was 6½ years old he was asked to complete a three-dimensional shape-sorting puzzle, the type which you would normally give to a child of 18 months to 2 years. This was not given in the classroom but in a private assessment room. He quickly became frustrated and agitated by the task. He could not figure out how the three-dimensional shapes in his hand could not fit into the seemingly obscure orifices in the posting ball, each attempt was a pure guess and, more often than not, incorrect. 'They don't match' he cried desperately. Then his learning support assistant quietly said, 'try the star shape', as soon as Isaac had been given this additional verbal prompt he could do it. From there on Isaac only needed a prompt indicating the name of the shape to match each object quickly and efficiently.

The information Isaac was receiving through his proprioceptors and sense of touch was not providing him enough information to recognise the three-dimensional shape. Despite having very good visual ability to recognise two-dimensional shapes, he required further sensory information and experience of depth perception to appreciate the qualities of three-dimensional objects.

Difficulties in form constancy also affect judgement of size, which in turn influences drawings, physical education, handwriting and mathematics.

Figure–ground discrimination

Visual figure–ground discrimination is the ability to visually attend to one object to the exclusion of other stimuli in the visual field. The 'figure' is the object focused upon, which accommodates the observer's visual *attention*, and the ground is the visual stimuli which remains in the background. When attention is shifted onto something different, the previous figure recedes into the background, and a new figure becomes the focus. Difficulties in visual figure–ground discrimination are common in children with dyspraxia and have a huge impact on the child's learning. For example, as a child is trying to observe a teacher demonstrate a practical mathematical experiment, concentration is required to observe the appropriate activity and auditory attention is required to hear instructions. The child with difficulties would easily be distracted by other stimuli in the environment. Children with visual figure–ground discrimination difficulties will often find soft play environments and busy party or club environments visually overwhelming.

Similarly auditory figure–ground discrimination is the selection and attention to specific sounds. This requires the ability to cut out noises, which may have little relevance to the subject being attended to. Difficulties in this make it very difficult for children to attend to a selected noise or voice, as all sounds will be of similar importance. Considerable effort will be required to differentiate the relevant sound. Children with auditory discrimination difficulties will seemingly 'switch off' and appear distracted or disinterested.

Both auditory and visual figure–ground discrimination require conscious choice and cognitive effort. If we wish to listen to a conversation in a crowded party, for example, we must make the effort to listen and look at the person involved in the conversation, any distractions would disrupt efforts to complete the exchange. It is therefore a dynamic act, and essential for any learning and interaction. The struggle to constantly maintain a focus can often leave a child exhausted. As a consequence the child may begin to daydream or become disruptive.

Such was the case with Adam.

At the age of 6 Adam struggled in his Year 1 class of twenty-seven pupils. He was a bright boy who battled to cope in many group situations. His problems were amplified when the school he attended gained funding to build two new classrooms. However this required the adaptation of the current building and necessitated two classes using a temporary Portakabin for a period of approximately nine months. Adam's class was involved in this temporary move. The majority of his peers were delighted as the Portakabin, despite being small, was cosy and warm, unlike many of the classrooms. Adam, on the other hand, was frustrated by the lack of space and 'echoing floors'.

Adam became increasingly agitated as the term progressed. He complained at the seeming increase in the number of classroom displays, which he found a continual source of distraction. He also complained of being 'too squashed' and the room being 'too noisy'. Adam particularly struggled with circle time, and was irritated by children sitting too close to him. He also grew frustrated by the need to listen carefully when the room seemed to echo around him. His initial reaction was to try to create more space around him on the carpet by pushing others out of the way with his feet or arms, and spreading his legs, and then if unsuccessful emitting high-pitched squeals which disrupted the whole group. The consequence was that Adam was removed from the class and given time-out in a deserted cloakroom area. Interestingly this immediately calmed him as in this area he was able to relax, enjoy the silence and prepare to enter the class again. Adam ultimately needed a calm, quiet environment in which to work. To help address his needs an area of the classroom was cordoned off with the introduction of a language booth borrowed from a nearby language school which was closing. Time in this area gave Adam the opportunity to focus, attend and learn without the need for time out of the classroom.

In this scenario, distorted figure–ground discrimination was not only having an effect on Adam's visual attention but also auditory discrimination. However, this is not the only area this influences in the child's educational curriculum. Distorted visual figure–ground perception can have a profound effect on reading, writing, physical education and maths.

When reading the child with dyspraxia will often start school reading relatively well, as the material used has few words, large font, and a specific picture connected to the words. As reading develops, so does the reading material; font reduces in size and more text is introduced to each page. It is at this point that the information on each page becomes overwhelming. A child may struggle to focus on the specific words and will become distracted by the previous line or words; they will therefore lose their place on the page easily.

Handwriting will be affected. Words written may merge with those on the previous line as the child is visually distracted by preceding sentences. In physical education the sound of a sports hall plus movement by a large class may present as overwhelming visual and auditory stimuli which will distress the child. In maths organisation of information will be influenced by the volume of information on the page. The child will present as being disorganised and easily distracted. Many children's games will prove too difficult as the child is unable visually to identify and organise specific features of activities such as jigsaw puzzles, word searches, find-it books and sorting games.

Position in space

Position in space is a further aspect of perception, which helps us to appreciate a sense of space and depth. It is the ability to perceive or appreciate our body position in relation to our environment. It requires an understanding of spatial concepts such as above, below, beneath, etc. and the appreciation of where things are placed in relation to a central figure.

It enables us to develop a 'body schema' or self-awareness, which helps us to know, for example, where our arms are in respect to our trunk, the position of our head in relation to our feet, the position of our pelvis in relation to our shoulder girdle, and so on. Awareness of these positions serves to provide us with a map or picture of how we think that we look. We develop a sense of body image and our position in space mainly through our proprioceptors which signal messages to our brain giving location information as to our exact limb position. This enables us to develop a sense of proportion and awareness of body symmetry and subsequent sidedness. We learn that we have a left-hand side and a right-hand side and that it is easier to perform certain tasks with one hand more than the other, so becoming aware of hand dominance. We also learn about the midline position and proximity of our head in relation to the floor.

In developing this awareness we are able to build an accurate picture of how we look and move. This feedback enables us to develop a self-image which helps us to dress, put on make-up, comb our hair and present in a socially acceptable manner. To demonstrate our intact body schema we can reproduce figure-drawings which, may not be masterpieces, but will represent the correct proportions of our body, sizing and key features in relatively accurate detail.

Many children with dyspraxia will have dysfunctional position in space and this will reflect in a poor understanding of self-image, poor appreciation of the body's proportions, and a lack of appreciation of laterality. Self-drawings will be immature

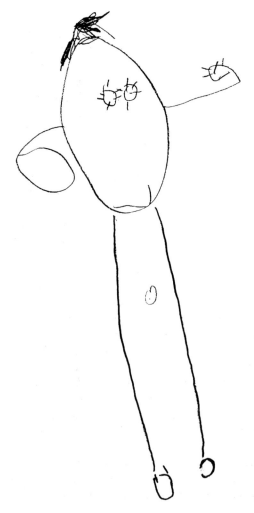

Figure 2.2 Self-drawing by John aged 8

and lacking in detail, and proportions may be erratic. The child may perceive himself differently from his peers and may be unaware that he appears different.

Inability to determine a true dominance or laterality will influence coordinated movements. The child may struggle to locate left and right, this will be reflected in orientation, and may enhance their uncoordinated appearance. Confused laterality will also affect letter orientation when writing with frequent letter reversals being apparent. Mirror-writing may occur or simply reversed letters may appear within words. The individual may start writing from the right side of the page and proceed to the left. Often young people with dyspraxia who have difficulties with position in space will continue to have orientation problems in adulthood, when, for example, learning to drive. They will find it difficult to not only coordinate the controls for driving but also to orientate between left and right. Map-reading becomes very problematic.

Spatial relationships

Spatial relationship is the ability to perceive the position of two or more objects in relation to self and in relation to one another. The ability to judge depth and distance requires an appreciation of a third dimension, and therefore is dependent upon adequate form constancy. It is also dependent upon an intact personal awareness of position in space. It also requires intact figure–ground discrimination to help determine foreground and background. In amalgamating these perceptual components together, it is possible to appreciate spatial relationships whereby a number of parts can be seen simultaneously, such as when watching a football match. In this example it is possible to observe the location of the ball while scanning the distances from the ball to surrounding players. In actuality, all parts are not seen simultaneously but are mentally scanned and organised in a way in which a whole picture is formed. This is a crucial skill for motor organisation, and enables a child to manoeuvre around a busy classroom without bumping into anything or anyone.

Children with dyspraxia experience difficulties judging distances and assessing space. This has significant consequences for motor coordination. For example when a child is asked to come to the front of the class following a period in circle time, they will struggle to judge the location of fellow pupils in relation to one another and will either step on a child's hand or foot, or bump into a nearby object. It appears that they are unable to see a clear pathway through. Subsequently the group is disrupted and more often than not, the child is reprimanded for 'choosing the wrong way'.

Climbing stairs can prove a struggle for children with spatial difficulties, particularly travelling downstairs, as the distance 'downhill' can appear considerably further than anticipated. Consequently many children with dyspraxia go downstairs with two feet to a stair, will cling onto a banister for help or will take to their bottoms.

These difficulties in judging distances are made worse when the child must move from the floor's surface. Activities such as walking along a low gym bench, climbing ropes or jumping over a horse using a springboard will be quite terrifying, and the child will be at risk from falling.

As distances are hard to assess, children with spatial relationship difficulties will prefer to be 'grounded'. This means that they will feel safer if situated on the floor. Physical education activities will appear frightening as a group of people move

together in varying directions. Often in the physical education lesson the child will either choose to sit on the floor, or will be found clinging to a wall or secure object.

This inability to judge physical space can also have repercussions outside the school environment. Consider the following example.

Helen was really excited to go on a school trip to Holy Island, in Northumberland. Before boarding the coach to return to school, time was given to allow the students to buy souvenirs in the local gift shops. The shops on the island were small and filled with a mass of memorabilia. In the doorway of one shop, Helen dropped her purse and was unable to judge the space around her to appreciate how she could bend down and pick the purse up. Instead she sat on the shop floor and reached out in order to locate the purse. In doing so she managed to knock a display of postcards to the floor. The shock of this caused her to stand up abruptly and she knocked down a rack of maps. The shopkeeper was irate and informed Helen how exasperated she was with her 'clumsiness'. Helen left the shop without any memento, embarrassed and humiliated. She returned to her coach, with all the happy thoughts of her day left behind in that gift shop.

This example demonstrates the extent to which dyspraxia can impact on self-confidence and self-esteem.

The inability to judge distances will also present in the child's handwriting. Sizing will be erratic and the child may leave too much or too little space between letters and words. This can cause writing to become indecipherable.

Mathematics is also affected by poor spatial planning on the page. Columns may be erratically placed causing calculation errors. Practical maths exercises and scientific experiments may be influenced by an inability to judge distances in order to position objects or mix solutions.

Outside in the playground the child may be unable to join in games such as football or hopscotch owing to an inability to position himself appropriately. Crossing the road will also prove a trial. This can seriously hinder a child's independence and cause parents considerable anxiety. Worries about future independence may lead to the child being overprotected and his activities limited.

Visual closure

The final aspect of perceptual development which is evident in children with dyspraxia is visual closure. Through visual closure we are able to predict whole objects fairly accurately despite only seeing a part. We can also determine an object if its outline is fragmented. Visual closure is demonstrated by our natural tendency to close gaps and complete unfinished forms, to see parts as wholes, and to supply missing information. This suggests that an object is made up of series of forms which when patterned together make a single entry. The face is a familiar example. To recognise a familiar face, each part is scanned and a pattern quickly forms to enable us to recognise a whole face. This ability allows us to recognise familiar faces even when the face is partially occluded with a hat, sun glasses or scarf. Our mind or memory supplies the missing features. This ability helps us to recognise objects and people quickly even though we may not have complete information.

Some children, though not all, with dyspraxia experience difficulties in this areas of perceptual development. It is more prevalent in children who have a concomitant pragmatic–semantic language disorder or a pervasive development disorder. However, in children with dyspraxia this presents in a number of ways. Such children may be unable to complete jigsaw puzzles as they are unable to see how parts can connect together. Dot-to-dot puzzles may prove difficult as they appear a mass of individual forms with seemingly little connections, letter shapes may fragment, for example the letter 'b' may be written as a 'I' and 'o' separate from one another. In the classroom items partly hidden within a room may be impossible to find as the 'whole' object cannot be perceived. The child may struggle to 'read' facial expressions which in turn can influence social skills and social behaviour.

Figure 2.3 Exercise in visual closure: can you identify the fragmented object?

Having described in detail the various components of perceptual development it is hoped that readers can now understand the profound impact that perception has to play on the child's motor coordination, and learning ability. More so we can now see how dysfunctional perception can distort a child's image of the world and can reap serious consequences for the child's learning, social acceptability and self-confidence. Indeed, the term perceptuo-motor dysfunction is a more accurate description of dyspraxia than has been previously realised. In identifying the various components which enable a child to perceive and make sense of his environment, it is possible to be very specific about the intervention offered, and in addressing the underpinning processes involved in perceptual and motor development, skills can be learned and generalised in a range and number of new and unfamiliar situations.

We now need to appreciate how motor-planning difficulties can impact on verbal skills and consider the presentation of a small proportion of children whose dyspraxia also affects their speech. It is appropriate that we include some of the issues related to what is commonly known as developmental verbal dyspraxia.

Developmental verbal dyspraxia

It was Morley, Court and Miller who in 1954, first applied the term dyspraxia to a child's speech difficulties. They highlighted:

> A defect of articulation which occurs when the movements of the muscles used for speech . . . appear normal for involuntary or spontaneous movements . . . but are inadequate for the complex and rapid movements used for articulation and reproduction of sequences of sounds used in speech.

However, while developmental verbal dyspraxia (also sometimes called developmental articulatory dyspraxia) is talked about as a condition in its own right, there is in fact a great deal of controversy as to whether it actually exists as a separate entity. In a recent article, Williams (2002) writes 'In published literature, there remains little agreement on terminology, symtomatology, diagnostic features and indeed on its very existence'.

Stackhouse (1992) is clear that speech features alone should not be used as a basis for diagnosis, but that the child should present with a number of deficits, i.e. clinical, linguistic, phonetic and cognitive, and that evidence of these deficits should be collected over time. In an article by Reeves (1996), verbal dyspraxia is described as 'marked difficulties in producing speech sounds and in sequencing them together in words'. This emphasises that, in a similar way to gross/fine motor development, it is the poor organisation and processing of relevant muscles which hinders speech production.

In verbal dyspraxia, expressive language is often delayed. This is due to a difficulty in making and coordinating the precise movements of the lips, tongue and palate required to produce speech. Voice production difficulties due to incoordination at the laryngeal level are also common. Stackhouse (1992) in a longitudinal study introduces Keith who she says 'was unable to adopt a whistle posture to command and yet could blow a kiss to his mother automatically'. This inability to perform actions on request is a curious feature of verbal dyspraxia.

Children will often (but not always) have both these types of dyspraxia concerned with speech and language (i.e. verbal and oral-motor). Some children (but not all) may be affected by both motor and verbal dyspraxia. It is then important that people are aware of the distinctions between them, because some theory and treatment concerned with motor dyspraxia may not be relevant or worthwhile for a child whose difficulties are predominantly with speech and language.

Williams (2002) further suggests that 'The fashion of giving a very specific diagnosis may well be changing. Instead of identifying categories and sub-categories of conditions, speech and language therapists may now describe the child's difficulties in general terms as a *developmental speech and language disorder*'. In this way the therapist can deal with the predominant feature at any particular time, as a child's strengths and weaknesses will change as they grow and develop.

It would seem, then, that there is a great deal of uncertainty relating to the condition but there is no doubt that the accurate and efficient acquisition of speech and language is central to being a competent social being. As Ayres (1979) suggests

> Talking, and in particular learning to talk, requires very complex motor planning. It requires the ability to initiate a motor act on one's own inner command. Then one must arrange the sequence of movements to make the sounds for a word, in one's brain one must decide which word follows which. Specific movements of the mouth, tongue and lips are needed for good articulation.
>
> (p. 120)

Developmental verbal dyspraxia is then, much more than a speech problem. Children with ongoing speech and language difficulties beyond the age of 5 years have shown to be at great risk of having literacy difficulties. So a child with speech and language difficulties will very often have educational difficulties also. Those problems may not be easily observable in the very young, whose speech can be inconsistent, but will become more apparent as more and more is expected of them.

As with motor dyspraxia, these children do not form a neat homogeneous group, and their needs, strengths and weaknesses will change as they grow and develop. Specialist speech and language therapy should be available, but rather than being exclusive it should be within the framework of the child's educational needs and take into consideration the compensatory strategies that a child has developed. It is reasonable to suggest that children with developmental verbal dyspraxia respond extremely well to appropriate support, but it must be remembered that even though their dyspraxic difficulties may not always be apparent they will remain throughout their adult lives. As Stackhouse (1992) suggests, adults with dyspraxia would benefit from a 'life-line'; the knowledge that there is someone to whom they can turn for help. It may be that children with verbal dyspraxia respond well to treatment that is offered, but they may well turn up in adult literacy classes later in life. 'It is impossible to make predictions about an individual's progress from the initial presentation of the condition. It would seem that the more pervasive and persisting the speech and associated problems, then the more limiting might be employment prospects' (p. 86).

It is extremely important that speech and language difficulties are identified as early as possible and that specialist provision is made in the form of speech and language assessment and therapy. As Daines et al. (1996) suggest: 'Language is a means of thinking about, and responding to, the world'. It is 'a powerful tool for learning'.

Despite the confusion and controversy (and lack of research), children do still obtain a diagnosis of developmental verbal dyspraxia, and it is with this in mind that we will go on to explore the clinical features and affects of this condition in the following chapters.

Chapter 3

Characteristics

Having described the main differences between the child with dyspraxia and his peers, it is useful to be aware of the key characteristics that children with dyspraxia display. However, it is also extremely important that not every child who trips over chairs or bumps into every available person is labelled 'dyspraxic'.

Readers should be aware that a child should display a cluster of these characteristics. If a teacher, parent or other carer is concerned that a child is displaying these features, they should observe the child for a period of time before rushing in and possibly subjecting the child to unnecessary assessments and the family to unneeded anguish. However, while teachers and carers should exercise caution, they should not turn a blind eye to developmental differences in children, as the earlier developmental dyspraxia is detected, assessed and diagnosed, the better for the individual concerned. To help identify children who exhibit features of dyspraxia it is worth considering the characteristics discussed in the following sections.

Pre-school characteristics

It is often difficult to identify dyspraxia in pre-school children owing to the variations in normal development. Often specific difficulties in motor coordination are not apparent, as complex activities such as riding a bike are often not mastered until the child is 5 or 6 years of age. Perceptual skills, which begin to develop at an early age are not mature until a child is 7 or 8 years old, and therefore difficulties in these are not as obvious as when the child reaches school age. Verbal dyspraxia may be more obvious as speech develops quite rapidly between the ages of 18 months and 5 years. However, pressure regarding speech production is not as intense in a family environment where parents and siblings can 'tune in' to the nuances of speech and the non-verbal signals given by a child struggling with speech production. Limited speech is therefore put down to immaturity, laziness, sibling communication and the use of competent non-verbal signals.

Consequently the characteristics seen in the pre-school child are subtler and easily mistaken for immaturity or lack of experience. However, it is useful to observe the child participating in the activities discussed in the following sections.

Running

Children with dyspraxia often run awkwardly with their lower legs splayed out at the knees and with an awkward gait, which will continue beyond the age of 5 years.

In particular it may be worth noting how the child initiates the running action, if the signal 'go' is called, is the child able to set off immediately or is there hesitation? When calling 'stop', is the child able to stop on cue or does he continue for a few steps? Does he have what is often termed an 'overflow of movements'? Further observation should note whether the child's running demonstrates a sense of rhythm, or whether the movement is awkward, heavy footed, with poor heel–toe strike as is the case with many children with dyspraxia.

Hopping

Hopping requires the ability to balance on either foot; this involves the sophisticated adjustment of a sensitive vestibular system plus motor coordination. In a pre-school child this develops gradually and by the age of 4 the child is able to balance on one leg and project up and down on that same leg to hop. We know that children with dyspraxia often have vestibular-processing difficulties, which impede balance. This has a bearing on the child's ability to hop, which is often not possible until the child is over 6 years old, and only after considerable practice. The ability to hop may seem an arbitrary skill, but in reality many daily tasks require a child to balance on one leg at a time, for example stair-climbing, climbing up a park slide, mounting a bike or tricycle, etc.

Ascending/descending stairs

Perceptual difficulties and an inability to balance on either leg may mean that the child with dyspraxia will struggle to step up and down stairs. Spatial difficulties effect how the child perceives the distance from one step to another, as the child's visual field is greater on the downward journey. It is not uncommon for a child to stumble when descending stairs and to misplace feet position. Stair descent can be stressful and cause a child considerable anxiety. Descent of moving stairs such as in an escalator can be too much to attempt especially if located in a busy shopping mall.

Sitting still

There are varying expectations, at pre-school level, regarding a child's attention level. Young children keen to explore their world seem to be constantly on the move, and never seem to sit still. However, as the child matures they are able to attend and concentrate for increasing periods of time. The ability to sit still and concentrate on a task may of course depend on the child's interest and motivation in the activity. What is often noticeable about the child with dyspraxia is their continued fidgeting even when absorbed in an activity such as watching TV. There are two theories as to why a child with dyspraxia does this. First, poor sensory regulation results in the child craving tactile stimulation in order to register his position in space. Second, there is a more recent suggestion that the child with dyspraxia continues to exhibit primitive reflexes which usually disappear either before or shortly after birth (Goddard, 1996). One reflex in particular, the spinal gallant reflex causes a child to squirm in response to any physical contact with the spine, consequently when a child places his back against the back of a chair, this reflex is stimulated causing the child to be restless.

Toilet-training

Children with dyspraxia often learn to use the toilet independently later than their peers do. This is due to poor sensation, which reduces the awareness, required to know when to use the toilet. Efficient personal hygiene after toileting is also delayed by the child's inability to manoeuvre the hands when these are positioned behind the child. Poor proprioception (knowing where the limbs are in relation to the body without the need for sight) limits manipulative skills to use toilet paper correctly. To accommodate this, children often resort to wiping from back to front rather than vice versa, increasing the risk of infection.

Calculating danger

The ability to judge distances is fundamental to safe actions. Unfortunately, as children with dyspraxia commonly have difficulties judging distances, they are unsafe in many childhood games. For example, they may jump from the highest point of a climbing frame or across a divide, which they cannot possibly clear. Judging the speed of traffic and distance across a road may also be limited. They may also be unable to assess the speed of a flying object when playing ball games and be vulnerable to injury. Poor sensation may expose the child to varying temperature changes and they may be unable to reflect upon whether they are too hot or too cold when playing outdoors. Consequently these children are at risk, and need boundaries and guidance to ensure their safety.

Regulating their emotions

Being unable to join in your peers' games can be immensely frustrating and humiliating for even the youngest child with dyspraxia. Simple tasks such as pulling up a zip, putting on a shoe, putting together a four-piece jigsaw, etc. can prove extremely difficult for the child with dyspraxia. Often the distress at not being able to succeed is suppressed and rears its head at seemingly inappropriate times. Often their reaction is a culmination of a number of struggles. As each day is a challenge to many children with dyspraxia and is accompanied by many accidents, reprimands and limited achievements, the consequences of this is an explosion of pent-up emotion which is expressed through tantrums, self-abuse, destructive behaviour, tears and noisy rages. A change in the day's routine can exacerbate these.

Manipulating toys

Manipulation of certain toys e.g. jigsaws, Duplo and other constructional toys will be difficult for many children with dyspraxia. This is due to poor fine-motor coordination and may not be apparent, as early play activities require gross movements. As the child matures, toys increase in complexity and demand more dexterity; difficulties in manipulation will therefore become more apparent.

Reaching milestones

Both health professionals and parents frequently use developmental milestones to monitor a child's progress. It is expected, for example, that a child will sit unaided at 6 months, crawl by 10 months and walk by 15 months (Sheridan *et al.*, 1997). Some milestones may be omitted, such as crawling, and the child might traverse from sitting to bottom-shuffling, through to walking without crawling. There is current debate about the significance of this on the child's development. In children with dyspraxia expected milestones are usually achieved but perhaps later than usual.

Following instructions

Parents and nursery teachers may feel that they are speaking a foreign language at times, as the child's response to questions seems to be unusually limited and delayed. This may be caused by the child attempting to absorb and organise the incoming information before responding or acting on it. It is one of the earliest signs of the child with dyspraxia's organisation and processing difficulties. A child with developmental verbal dyspraxia will have considerable difficulties responding to questions due to limited expressive language.

Coping with various sensory stimuli

As a young child matures, he grows to appreciate and distinguish between the various sensory experiences in his environment. These experiences enable children to extend their knowledge of the environment and begin to select or favour certain stimuli over others. This can be seen when feeding young children solids, an often difficult time for many parents. Their response to new textures, tastes and smells will either lead them to seek or reject certain foods. Likewise various tactile experiences will arouse curiosity and interest. Early introduction to a variety of sensory experiences is the goal of many babies' toys, which often incorporate sound, touch and visually stimulating elements. If we consider tactile experiences in particular, very early in a child's development certain textures such as polystyrene chips, dry grass, or Hessian carpets, are often uncomfortable, whereas fleece blankets, crinkly paper and porridge may be more pleasurable. Many children with dyspraxia are either overly sensitive to certain sensations or may lack sensitivity. Consequently many items of clothing, food textures and tastes might be too sensitive for the child to cope with. This results in the child removing clothing, becoming distressed at having dirty hands, and becoming a fussy eater.

Children with dyspraxia may also be hypersensitive to noise, and prefer a quiet environment or shy away from large group play in kindergarten. Parties may be too overwhelming and uncomfortable. Sudden loud noises may cause alarm and distress. The opposite can also be true, the child being under sensitive to sensory information.

Accident-prone

Most pre-school children experience their fair share of accidents before entering full-time education. This is due to developing coordination while increasing in confidence to explore the exciting world that they live in, it is also natural for children at this age to test boundaries and their own limitations, this leads to a number of bumps, bruises and occasionally more serious injuries. However, the child with dyspraxia has more accidents than the average child and seems to be forever tripping, spilling, bumping, misplacing and dropping things.

Limited speech

A child begins to use simple words by 12 months, by 18 months the child has acquired ten to twelve words if not more. By 2 years simple sentences are forming and the child is able to request and respond in a simple manner. A child with dyspraxia may have delayed speech production, and when he is able to vocalise, this is jumbled, unclear or immature. It should be noted that parents become accustomed and attuned to the speech of their own children and so may not always notice the difference in speech and language abilities, especially if the affected individual is their first child.

Feeding difficulties

Some children with verbal dyspraxia may also have difficulties in sucking, feeding, chewing and swallowing. These may be reported at a very early age, but links with dyspraxia may not emerge until further characteristics are noted.

Key Stages 1 and 2

The diagnosis of dyspraxia is more commonly given when the child begins full-time education. It is at this time, that parents and teachers realise that certain behaviours cannot be accredited to boisterousness, immaturity and the home experiences. The structure of the National Curriculum requires each child, from Key Stage 1 onward, to obtain a level of dexterity in order to write, draw, produce calculations, create, demonstrate and construct. It also demands gross motor ability in order to move independently at various speeds, dance, play games and extend the body's potential to fulfil the objectives set out in the National Curriculum Physical Education Strategy. In addition socially appropriate behaviour is expected with relationships being extended, and roles being respected. It is at this point that the child with dyspraxia will present differently and the extent of his difficulties will become more evident. The following characteristics will emerge:

Poor handwriting

One of the significant features of *all* school-aged children with dyspraxia is evidence of poor handwriting skills. These children have significant difficulties in many aspects of this complex skill from holding the pencil appropriately to positioning the writing on the page. It is one of the main areas in which a child becomes conscious that their abilities are lacking. Handwriting becomes a chore and a source of increased frustration. Considering that so much of the child's school day involves handwriting-related activities, we can see how this is an area which has the greatest effect on the child's self-confidence and self-esteem.

Poor drawing abilities

During the foundation stage of a child's early education experience, considerable emphasis is placed on multi-sensory activities; this incorporates much creativity using paint, crayons, model building and crafts. This continues throughout the child's education with an expectation that the child's creativity will demonstrate increasing skill, inventiveness and ingenuity. However, the child with dyspraxia will not only struggle with the fine motor control required to write effectively, but will also labour to control pencils/crayons to draw effectively. Dysfunctional perception, particularly poor form constancy and position in space will seriously impede the child's ability to reproduce three-dimensional objects, proportions will also be erratic and self-drawings will be very basic and often disjointed. A sample of this is provided by Figure 3.1.

Skipping

In the foundation and Key Stage 1 of the National Curriculum the ability to skip is encouraged. Initially this is presented within physical education classes as an alternative way to move. This requires the ability to hop, project forward and move in a rhythmical manner. In children with dyspraxia skipping appears awkward, heavy, lacks rhythm and has restricted propulsion. The more complex, fun activity of skipping with a rope requires even more multifaceted skills and for this the child has to perpetuate several different motions at once. The child must be able to rotate the rope, judge the speed of the rope in relation to the feet, respond by jumping at the correct time, and repeating this pattern of movement in a rhythmic way. This therefore requires coordination, spatial organisation and patterned movement, abilities which children with dyspraxia often do not have.

Messy eaters

Prior to starting school it can be acceptable to have unusual or messy eating habits, as often this is not subject to public scrutiny. It is therefore more acceptable for children to reject knives and forks in favour of fingers, and choose foods, which are easy to control. At school, however, the child is exposed to social and cultural norms and expectations as to what is the most appropriate and acceptable way to eat food. This usually involves the coordinated use of knife and fork, closure of the mouth when eating, restriction of speaking when the mouth is full and occasional social conversation and eye contact with others during the course of the meal. Many children with dyspraxia will find the efficient use of cutlery difficult to master and may resort to using fingers. They may eat 'badly' (i.e. with mouths open) and have a tendency to spill things. They are usually slow to complete a meal. This may become a situation where the child is teased and reprimanded. Poor self-awareness will influence oral control and the concentration required to control cutlery may be at the expense of social courtesy. Consequently the child may either avoid formal meals such as school dinners as much as possible, and snack on easy-to-eat foods which are often unhealthy.

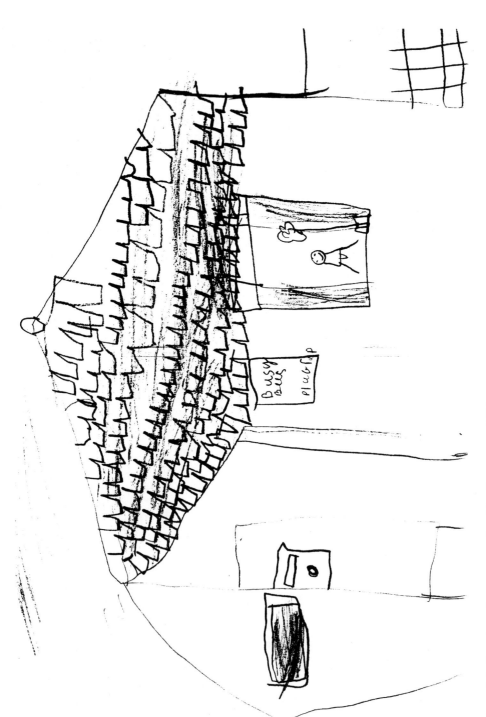

Figure 3.1 Drawing of a nursery school by Gemma aged 7½

Slow or poor at dressing

Before school entry, the pressure to dress quickly and smartly depended heavily on a mum or carer's agenda. If speed were required, a helping hand could be given, if not, comfortable clothes could be worn at leisure. At school, it is another story. The allocation of an appointed uniform ensures homogeneity among children. However, this usually includes a blouse or shirt containing stiff collar, starched cuffs and a series of 1 centimetre buttons, a tie whose soul purpose is decoration, regulation skirts or trousers, merged together with matching woolly jumper or cardigan with even more buttons! At least once or twice a week this has to be removed quickly and replaced with elasticised shorts and polo-shirts or t-shirts to undertake a forty-five minute PE session, following which the replacement of the aforementioned uniform will be required. To a child with reasonable coordination and intact perceptual skills this is an acquired skill, but for the child with dyspraxia it is nothing short of a public nightmare. Poor coordination impaired body image, poor laterality and pressure of time all add to this difficult task making it almost 'painful' to watch the child's efforts and many teachers of young children resort to doing it for them. This is less acceptable with an older child, and they can be subject to ridicule.

Inability to generalise skills

The inability to transfer skills, or learn non-habitual tasks can limit the child with dyspraxia. A child, who has learned to catch a ball for example, may be completely flustered if a beanbag is thrown instead. The skills that other children seem to learn almost automatically have to be taught to a child with dyspraxia until they become habitual. The extent to which skills are generalised will heavily depend upon how they were introduced in the first place. Often skills introduced, rehearsed and practised in one location may not be transferred into another situation or may not extend to help with other skills. This is often more apparent with social behaviour than physical behaviour, for example if a certain code of conduct is taught at home, i.e. a method of clearing crockery away after a meal, this may not be utilised when in a school diningroom, where crockery has to be carried on a tray and placed in a selected area. Skills, which are taught by addressing the underpinning processes, are more effective in ensuring that a skill is generalised. For example, handwriting can be improved with practice through repetitive movements, though this is limited to the movements repeated, but when the various aspects of handwriting are addressed, i.e. grasp of the pencil, hand–eye coordination, form development, etc., improvement is generalised into, not only writing but, drawing and other functional activities.

Distractible

As children enter Key Stage 1, they are introduced to a structured curriculum which requires a minimum one hour of literacy and one hour of numeracy each day, in addition to other subjects. The volume of information which a child is expected to absorb requires considerable attention and concentration. As the majority of children with dyspraxia have visual and auditory figure–ground discrimination difficulties, prolonged attention can require enormous effort which many children are not able to sustain, consequently they may begin to daydream, go off at a tangent, or become agitated and disruptive.

Physical coordination

The physical incoordination identified in the pre-school child increases as activities involving balance, dexterity and movement increase in complexity. This is especially evident in PE and in playground activities. For example, spatial difficulties will restrict the child's ability to move around apparatus, and will hinder accurate judgement of distance when playing team games.

A tendency to be the 'class clown'

From an early age children learn how to promote their abilities and hide their inadequacies. Children with dyspraxia are acutely aware that they find things more difficult than their peers do. Responses to this vary but 'clowning around' is a great way of getting attention and winning friends. It is also an excellent way to irritate the teacher enough to be removed from the situation and is a tactic often used to avoid doing certain subjects which may prove particularly difficult.

It must be noted that some children adopt other strategies to compensate for their inadequacies; feigning illness is very common and is more difficult to assess. Parents will also respond to physical complaints and absences from school can result.

As a practicing occupational therapist, I have also seen children reproduce chunks of writing taken verbatim from a series of books, which together gives the appearance of a considered piece of work. I have also seen a child use brilliant dramatic 'made-up' events to avoid a subject. I have seen many parents undertake the child's homework and for this to be presented as if it were the child's, to avoid rebuke for slow work. I have even caught children messing about in cloakrooms to avoid sessions involving writing. All these examples demonstrate the profound psychological effect dyspraxia has on the child's self-esteem and confidence.

Planning and organising difficulties

In order for the child to get through much of the work required under the National Curriculum, effective time management is required. This requires the child to attend, concentrate, and then undertake the required work in the allotted time. We know that children with dyspraxia have difficulties in organising themselves and planning their time, and will spend some time before each task developing a strategy for achievements. It can appear that the child is messing about or using delaying tactics, and this may well be the case, but we need to observe carefully whether delays in commencing or completing work is part of the child's processing difficulties. For children with dyspraxia, seemingly simple tasks appear to take a great deal of thought and then are often executed inefficiently. These children often copy what they see rather than plan and organise it for themselves.

Sometimes it may appear that the child has a poor memory as they struggle to recall information or instructions. Rather than this being a specific problem with memory it is more to do with organising information in the form of an effective action plan which is the problem. Consequently, if the child is given a series of instructions, these may become disorganised in their planning and the child may appear confused about what they need to tackle first.

Accident-prone

The tendency to tumble, knock and trip continues to be a feature of the child with dyspraxia. The coordination difficulties experienced during the pre-school years cannot now be put down to immaturity or boisterous behaviour. There may even be an increase in the number of accidents, as the child now must reserve his movements to the confines of often cluttered classrooms. This is even more significant during playtime when a child may have to spend some time in a restricted area with several classes together.

Tendency to seek the company of much younger children or adults

One of the consequences of spending time with large numbers of children especially during playtime is an increased awareness of personal movement abilities. This is especially noticeable in boys who may find the playtime activities of their peers require good coordination and perceptual skills of the highest order (e.g. football). Younger children do not ask as much of them and adults are often safer still. It should be noted that although these children can often be seen as isolated or on the periphery of the main action, it is not because they are unsociable, but more to do with their awareness of their limitations.

Delayed ability to ride a bike

The ability to ride a bike requires very complex skills. The child must balance on a device no wider than 4 centimetres while simultaneously propelling the legs, stabilising the arms and looking around for a clear pathway. The majority of children are able to achieve this complex skill by the age of 6 or 7. Despite its complexity, the ability to ride a bike is very important to children's friendships, as this is often a shared leisure pursuit. Children with dyspraxia have additional problems of coordinating reciprocal leg movements against gravity, while having poor assessment of speed, dysfunctional awareness of space and distance, and they may also be unable to separate out the movements of legs and arms; hence steering is affected. Many children with dyspraxia may avoid two-wheeler bikes altogether, but this may go unnoticed for a while as they may always opt for the push-along toys or scooter-type vehicles.

Extreme levels of motor activity

Children with dyspraxia are often unable to regulate their movements. They may be both very excitable and may hand flap in a way that is expected of a much younger child, or be extremely slow to respond to actions as they struggle to conceptualise the requested activity.

Slow to complete work

We have explained earlier how children with dyspraxia struggle to conceptualise and plan activities and it is these organisational difficulties which slow down the child's work. This can often be mistaken for delaying strategies or avoidance tactics, which can be very frustrating to the child's teacher, and this may well be the case especially if the child is confused as to how to implement the request. It is worthwhile checking the child's understanding of the task by simple questions relating to his ideas and plans for completing the task. As children progress through Key Stages 1 and 2, increasing demands are placed on them in respect of output, complexity of cognitive processing and refined movement. With the increased demands, problems in organisation become more apparent and work slows down. This is particularly evident with the volume of handwriting expected. The majority of children with dyspraxia will find it difficult to complete a piece of work in the allocated time.

Difficulties with toileting

Difficulties in cleaning oneself after toileting provide a continuing concern with personal hygiene. Poor proprioception continues to limit the child's ability to wipe from front to back and often children suffer from urinary infections and problems with personal hygiene. As a consequence they may start to become very self-conscious and try not to use the toilet at school, which again increases risk of infections and constipation. The child might find it impossible to agree to sleep-overs at friends for fear of toileting difficulties.

Certain children leave out sounds in words

Children who have oral dyspraxia as well as motor dyspraxia will occasionally omit certain sounds in words, i.e. 'mammy' sounds like 'mmmee', or they may change the word completely, i.e. mummy becomes 'mooz'. This can make speech difficult to follow. It can also create an avenue for teasing by others.

Voice tone can be erratic

Many children with dyspraxia will have difficulties controlling speed rhythm, intonation and loudness of speech. These children often seem to lack a volume control, which can be irritating in a classroom situation, and cause friction in social situations. Requests to read out loud may be greeted with groans from the rest of the class as the child may read in a laboured lifeless manner.

Speech intelligibility

Children with oral dyspraxia will struggle to produce planned speech. Speech will often deteriorate the more he tries to say. The effort of the speech means that they may start quite clearly but may have lost their listener by the time they have finished. Speech is also affected by pressure. Certain words or phrases may be produced automatically in spontaneous situations where the child is not 'put on the spot'. The same words may not be able to be produced on command for example if someone says 'what did you say?'. The child may appear to grope around for the right words and consequently may grimace as he struggles to control the oral–motor patterns required for effective speech.

Reading difficulties

Children with oral dyspraxia may also have reading difficulties which differ to those who have motor but not oral dyspraxia. Children with oral difficulties may have concerns regarding phonetic reproduction of words. This is particularly evident in words, which have the same sound but different spelling such as hair/hare, and there/their. This can impact on the acquisition of literacy skills particularly spelling and reading.

Children with dyspraxia, which does not affect speech, may also have difficulties with reading as they progress through to Key Stage 2. This is due to visual perception difficulties particularly visual figure–ground discrimination where too much information on a page can make the font appear blurred and confused.

Key Stages 3 and 4

By the time a child with dyspraxia has reached the age of 11 and has transferred into secondary education, they have usually adopted many strategies to attempt to mask their difficulties. Often certain tasks are avoided completely for fear of failure or to cover difficulties in specific areas. Refusal to attempt certain tasks can get the child the reputation of being stubborn and difficult. Many children have learned how to compensate well and therefore their common characteristics may not be overtly apparent. However, the characteristics discussed in the following sections may still be noted.

Clumsiness is less evident

At this age many young people who were previously 'sporty' and 'active' now have *choice*. They have options for leisure activities; consideration of a range of subjects; and sometimes, choices of activities within the PE class. The acute awareness of their lack of physical prowess evokes many children with dyspraxia to develop expert excuses for opting out of any activity, which might amplify their difficulties, e.g. many boys choose rugby rather than football, as it requires less motor control and falls and bumps are more acceptable.

Sometimes puberty can be a positive experience for many children with dyspraxia, as the increased rate of physical growth, renders *all* young people 'clumsy' and self-conscious.

Speed of handwriting is limited

During Key Stage 2 there is an expectation that all children have developed a fast, fluent, cursive handwriting style so that they are able to use this as an 'automatic' means of recording information and presenting knowledge. By the time a child reaches the age of 9 there is no mention of handwriting on the National Curriculum Literacy Strategy with the assumption that children will be proficient at writing at this stage. This supposition continues into Key Stages 3 and 4 with the expectation that writing speed will increase with practice in preparation for examinations. However, this is not the case for many children particularly those with dyspraxia who have struggled, and will continue to labour with handwriting throughout their remaining school years. Many children may have been introduced to word processors as alternatives to writing but those who have not, face ridicule and frustration at not being able to keep up with recording information at the expected pace. Comments about poor presentation skills are common; this says nothing about the child's effort, but lowers self-confidence and self-esteem.

Social isolation

This can be a *huge* area of concern in adolescence. Children with dyspraxia are usually sociable individuals who are unable to keep up with or compete with their peers. However poor hygiene, slow processing of information, disorganisation and poor timekeeping can often impact on friendships. Certain behaviours can influence peer relationships, for example difficulties adjusting voice tone, inability to whisper or speak quietly, raucous laughter at moderate humour, overt gestures and gesticulation; all result in the child lacking 'street cred'. Consequently the child can become quite isolated, or have only one or two friends with an equally 'uncool' reputation. This can often leave children vulnerable to bullying.

A child with oral dyspraxia may be increasingly isolated due to his poor speech and difficulty with intelligibility. Acute self-consciousness may severely handicap conversation and deterioration in learned speech may be noted.

Preoccupation with certain topics or subjects

Occasionally it might be noted that certain children have a curious interest in a specific topic or subject. This may give the appearance of almost 'obsessional' interest as seen in children with one of the autistic spectrum disorders. However the preoccupation witnessed in children with dyspraxia is more to do with finding something they *can* do, which they become consumed by.

Motor in coordination persists

Children with dyspraxia are often heard before seen as their heavy gait or shuffle characterises their arrival. Often teachers note that the child has a real fear of moving between classes during the school day. At this time up to 1,000 pupils are expected to move around the school simultaneously. More often than not, the child is late for lessons and is often seen struggling with stairs and confused by all the movement.

Poorly organised

Many young people with dyspraxia are noticed by their slightly dishevelled appearance. They will often arrive at the wrong place at the wrong time, and will regularly lack something required for certain lessons. In their free time their choice of clothes can be ill-fitting, poorly coordinated or clothes worn back to front.

Personal hygiene may still be difficult

This is often overlooked when considering the needs of these young people. If children are unable to cleanse themselves adequately by secondary school age it will become a social problem, as they will smell. Hygiene can be particularly problematic for girls with dyspraxia on commencement of their menstrual periods, as the management of a sanitary towel in a confined school toilet can be a coordination nightmare.

May suffer more extreme behavioural difficulties

They almost certainly will do if their difficulties have not been acknowledged and supported by the time they get to secondary school. Children may become disaffected with a reluctance to even try. They have spent a great deal of their school career in a state of frustration and failure.

Inconsistent learning performance

The psychological impact of dyspraxia is more evident during Key Stages 3 and 4. The child's confidence and self-esteem will acutely affect their daily performance. Therefore they will often be able to do something one day but not the next. Teachers need to be acutely aware of patterns of behaviour to determine whether the child is being bullied. Successive failures may take their toll and the child may not be physically or psychologically able to put the effort into their work on a consistent daily basis. These children are in danger of quickly experiencing motivational 'burnout'.

These characteristics describe some of the behaviours typically seen in many children with dyspraxia. Worried teachers should always consider environmental and social factors when they are observing/assessing children in their care.

Screening

Photocopy the checklist on the following pages to help you to identify whether the child you are concerned about may have dyspraxia. However, the importance of a comprehensive assessment and correct diagnosis cannot be overemphasised.

Pre-school checklist

Characteristics	yes	no
Crawled later than 10 months		
Learned to walk later than 18 months		
Unable to run without frequent falls		
Unable to hop on one leg by 5 years		
Difficulty sitting still		
Slow to achieve toilet training (3½ years or more)		
Unaware of danger		
Frequently falls over apparently minor obstacles		
Seems to be slow when processing instructions		
Avoids fine-motor activities such as Lego		
Unable to piece together jigsaw puzzles		
Struggles to post three-dimensional shapes in a posting box/ball		
Hates the feel of clothes against skin (woolly jumpers are particularly irritating)		
Accident-prone		
*may have poor speech		
Poor dressing skills		
Cannot use a knife and fork		
Play appears boisterous		
Prefers tasks such as watching TV but tends to be fidgety when doing so		
May skip around on tip-toes		

Key Stages 1 and 2 checklist

Characteristics	yes	no
Poor handwriting		
Poor drawing skills		
Unable to skip (not rope-skipping)		
Difficulty dressing and undressing for PE		
Messy eater; misses mouth and is reluctant to use a knife and fork		
Fearful or over boisterous in PE		
Concerned when using apparatus in PE		
Switches off in class		
Walks down stairs with two feet to each step		
Poor ball-catching skills		
Poor targeting skills		
Unable to jump with two feet together		
Unable to hop		
Seems slow to plan activity after being given instructions		
Erratic organisation		
Trips easily		
Accident prone		
Tends to be 'adopted' by younger peers		
Difficulties riding a bike		
Slow plodding gait (heavy-footed)		
Slow to complete work		
Unable to clean self properly after using the toilet		
*poor speech (those with oral dyspraxia)		
*speech deteriorates when 'put on the spot' (those with oral dyspraxia only)		
Tendency to be loud (struggles to talk in a whisper)		
Reading ability declines		

Key Stages 3 and 4 checklist

Characteristics	yes	no
Handwriting legibility remains poor		
Speed of handwriting is slow		
Three-dimensional drawings are difficult to achieve		
Child struggles with the layout of calculations in mathematics		
Concern seen when classes move at the end of each school period		
Continues to hold banister when descending stairs		
Avoids certain sports, i.e. team games such as football, netball		
Very self-conscious		
Behaviour may be disruptive or alternately child may become increasingly socially isolated		
Child may appear to have only one or two key interests, i.e. computers, food, chess		
Child is vulnerable to bullying		
Dress sense can be irregular (non-matching)		
Personal hygiene can be poor		
Continues to be accident prone		
Organisation is erratic with equipment or work being frequently lost		
Organisation of work is irregular (no logical order)		
Social skills are poor, i.e. lack of eye contact, incoherent speech, poor initiation of conversation, limited awareness of conversational rules		
Learning influenced by psychological state, i.e. low self-esteem may hinder output		
Avoidance of certain fine-motor activities, i.e. needlework, woodwork, design technology		

Chapter 4

The impact of dyspraxia

It is difficult to overestimate the impact of dyspraxia on a child's life at home and in the classroom. However, it is often difficult to articulate the impact in a meaningful way, because it can at times be so subtle. This makes it difficult to recount individual incidences in isolation without making them seem trivial. However, it is the accumulation of many individual differences, which makes them significant on a daily basis. It is fair to say that the impact is ongoing, far-reaching and lifelong. For a person with dyspraxia the fine-tuning in their lives, if you like, is missing. They tend to execute everything in a lengthy, cumbersome and often immature way, and so it is a whole series of little 'misfortunes' or 'near misses' that can make life so frustrating for them and the people they are closest to.

We have looked at the complexities of dyspraxia in former chapters and by now you should be getting some idea of the reasons behind the dilemma we recounted in the introduction of the little boy who defecated in the classroom. The difficulties that these children experience are complex and in many situations they have little choice but to join in with what is being asked even when they know it is impossible for them to be successful. The world is a puzzling place for them, because the way in which they do things, and the difficulties they incur is normal life to them. They have no experience of how others perceive the world and must surely wonder why they seemingly struggle with the things that others seem to do in an effortless way. Few of us have call to consider the complexities of speaking, dressing, using a knife and fork or riding a bike. Our children just seem to absorb these things and learn them almost as a matter of course. And indeed most of them do, it is what normal development allows them to do. It is only when these skills are compromised by a condition such as dyspraxia that parents, teachers, and the individuals themselves begin to realise that executing these skills is not a matter of course for everybody. Each new task and skill is a thing that really needs to be broken down into achievable steps, taught and retaught and practised if they are to be conquered and become habitual. Much as other children learn to play a musical instrument, the individual with dyspraxia has to practise and learn 'doing' and 'being' over and over again if they are to reach any level of competence. Few of us are taught how to be parents let alone to teach things that other families seemingly take for granted.

It should also be remembered that dyspraxia is a hidden disability, there are no obvious signs of difficulty, no sympathy votes, no desperation to help or understand. So children and families face prejudice and usually inappropriate judgement on a daily basis. The 'tuts' in the supermarket, the stares in the park take their toll.

Helen recalls:

I have become so tired with people tutting at my son in the supermarket, or looking at me like I am some kind of unfit mother that I have taken to carrying a pack of leaflets about dyspraxia around with me. Each person that 'tuts' is met by a leaflet being thrown their way!

We are assuming that the affected child's family is empathic and keen to understand, but this is not always the case. If the child's difficulties are not recognised or dismissed as bad behaviour at home, then he may find himself in a downward spiral, as his parents and siblings tire of his seeming thoughtlessness and stupidity. At school a similar picture can prevail, and it may now come as no surprise to discover that children with unrecognised dyspraxic difficulties are at great risk of behavioural difficulties, truancy or, worse, exclusion.

Even in the most supportive of environments a child with dyspraxia may be irritating and exhausting. One has to imagine living with a child who at perhaps 11 or 12 years old seems unable to do anything without continual and repetitive prompting. If speech and language is affected and the child remains a non-reader at this age, on top of the prompting a parent has to endure a continual barrage of questioning as the child tries to make sense of his world. Every answer is met with a 'what?' as the child plays for time to process the information he is being given. Many of the questions asked will be the same, but the child needs the constant repetition to file the information into his long-term memory. Many of you will have experienced life in a foreign country and the frustration of not being able to follow what is being said and not being able to read directions or advertisements. This must be comparable to life as a non-reader in our culture, which places a great deal of importance on literacy from a very early age. The individual becomes excluded from his cultural and social world by illiteracy.

So, to illustrate those little examples that may seem trivial in isolation, we now have a parent, unable to think because of the constant questioning, as well as being the interpreter in their child's world. Consider that on top of this in the middle of cooking the evening meal a mother's 12-year-old child calls for assistance in the toilet. He has tried to cleanse himself, and in so doing has used an entire roll of toilet paper and blocked the toilet. His brother wants to use the toilet 'now!'. She has to leave what she is doing to attend to him and the plumbing, and at the same time she may have other children requiring her attention and be feeling guilty about her lack of attention to their needs.

Imagine taking your children to the cinema, and one of them asking constant questions throughout the film because they cannot follow the speedy dialogue. Even worse, he asks ten minutes into the film if it has nearly finished and starts requesting loudly that he wants to go when the other children want to stay. Imagine the child who lacks the confidence to attend any clubs or events because at 12 years old they may be functioning at around age 7. Unaware of the child's difficulties, the group leader will usually have unrealistic expectations of the child's ability and understanding.

Many families find themselves in these circumstances and this is usually with little or no respite for them, or for the child or the siblings of the child who will often find their brother or sister embarrassing or an irritation.

To add to these ongoing pressures, many parents are asked to be therapists. These children are exhausted by the end of a school day, only to be faced by another session of 'work' by a mother who feels she must help the child to do better. The pressure on these families can escalate into worrying or damaging proportions.

Leigh said:

I so much want to go on a long walk with my family without my son tiring so quickly, and without worrying about him falling onto the road or off a narrow path. I long to have a family bike ride, or to go to a park without him feeling inadequate or wanting to use the apparatus that the park ordains he is too old for. I long to go to the cinema and manage to see the whole film, and not bring my son out in anger while his brother cries because his afternoon has been ruined. I long to do the things other families do sometimes, and I really long for a break from it all. For someone to ask me how I am, and to realise that sometimes I am struggling.

Elisa says:

It took me two years to teach my son to do his seatbelt up in the car, and a further year for him to do it without prompting. I couldn't understand what was happening. I then discovered the difficulties relating to visual perception. Doing up a seatbelt seems like such a simple task, but it includes the need for good body awareness, the ability to cross the midline, good fine-motor skills and being able to do something without visual cues. It is a very complex task when it is broken down into its individual components. Imagine what learning to write must be like!

These examples are given with thought. It may seem that we should all feel sorry for the mothers of these children who are under a great deal of pressure on a daily basis. This is not why this is written. However, these mothers' voices are important as they ring with the tones of people under pressure and it is for teachers and other professionals to realise that families which include a member with dyspraxia are often subjected to pressures that other people simply never have to consider. We should also consider that parents themselves may also have a specific learning difficulty, which will impact on the way that they are able to cope with the day-to-day struggles of their child.

It is then important that 'extra work' is given with caution and with some degree of forethought. Is the work really necessary? Can it be incorporated into the school day? It may simply be that the teacher needs at times to empathise with the mother before handing her something else to do.

If this is a minute taster of the impact on the mother and family we must also consider the impact this has on the child with dyspraxia. Children with dyspraxia have often faced pressures other children don't have to, before they have even walked through the school gate. Perhaps the child has wet the bed, perhaps he couldn't make himself understood, and perhaps he spilled his cereals, or put his shoes on the wrong feet again and senses his mother's frustration. Imagine being subjected to constant 'tuts' from adults and constant jibes from your siblings. Imagine what it is like not being able to wipe your bottom adequately at 12 years of age. Imagine what it feels like to not be able to read or to miss the point of all the jokes. Imagine what it is like to have endured a day at school when everyone around you seems to find everything they do much easier than you do. To have been sitting on the low-ability table when you are busting with ideas and answers but are unable to organise your thoughts to enable you to release examples of your intelligence into the wider world. Imagine setting out with an idea in mind only to find that the end result bears no resemblance to the initial concept. Imagine being left alone at playtime because your peers think you come from another planet.

This may seem to be overly negative and unrealistic, but it adequately sums up the reality for a lot of people with dyspraxia and it can be hard. Of course it is not like this for all people with dyspraxia, but if we can make a difference to just one person who is experiencing this negativity about himself, then surely we have a duty to make that difference.

On a less gloomy note, we must also consider the positive benefits of living or working with a child who is dyspraxic. These are children with a seemingly undentable tenacity, and who face a great deal of prejudice and discrimination with courage and patience. When you have watched a child struggle with almost everything they attempt to do, the smallest achievement is cause for celebration. When another child chooses to be with them it makes you glow with pride. When you have been so frustrated with the child's inability to understand, when you have felt like screaming with exasperation (or have indeed screamed) and the child comes through it all with a glowing smile it takes your breath away.

When a family comes through the trauma of having a child diagnosed with special needs, and when they can accept him for what he is and can encourage him to be proud of the differences that make him who and what he is, then it is true to say that they can reflect on what truly remarkable people individuals with dyspraxia are. Not heroic, not to be pitied but to be recognised for the truly exceptional individuals they are. There are many people who would buckle under the weight of what a child with dyspraxia has to carry and endure. View them with a degree of admiration but most importantly recognise their difficulties and accept them for what they are.

The impact of dyspraxia is far-reaching, it does not only affect the individual concerned, but it affects their relationships with their family members (and the relationships between those members). It touches all those people with whom they come into contact. It raises barriers that other people rarely have to negotiate and it adds pressures that others do not usually bare. It should make you stop and think about your part within that child's world and, it is hoped, make you reflect on your own practice. It is important to be aware of how privileged we are to be able to help them demonstrate their remarkable qualities.

Marilyn said:

There is nothing like witnessing the success of someone who has struggled to achieve something for so long. As parents, we all like to think that our children are happy and successful. We glow with pride when they have done something exceptional, or when they wear a 'good work' badge, or are asked to take the lead in the school play. However, when you have a child who finds most things difficult to achieve with ease, when they are successful, you are simply fit to burst. Seeing the success in their face and watching them grow with every small step forward is a feeling that can't be expressed in words. It is simply magical.

A teacher's voice:

Mrs Atkinson recalls a child with verbal dyspraxia in her primary class. His speech was extremely difficult to follow, but she always took the time to ask him to repeat what he said, crouched down to his level and looked interested in what he was trying to impart. She remembers feeling that she couldn't ask him to say something again when she had asked him four times already. Looking and feeling increasingly desperate she floundered a little until the child stepped towards her and gave her a hug. As if to say 'it doesn't matter, you have at least tried'. The teacher commented how much 'bigger' than her that little boy was. Even without the ability to make himself understood verbally, the child was forgiving and understanding of the teacher's frustration.

Part II

Facilitating learning in an inclusive setting

Chapter 5

Inclusion must be a state of mind

Before we begin to explore the very positive strategies that can be put in place to support children with dyspraxia in a mainstream classroom, we would like to touch on the subject of attitude. Successful inclusion really requires an attitude of motivation and acceptance. Teachers have got to want to support these children and to steer them towards reaching their own potential.

Inclusion is a word that is very much in fashion in education and a great deal has been written about it in recent years. Legislative documents, Acts of Parliament, books and memos direct us towards good practice and ways of 'creating' inclusive schools and eventually an inclusive society. However it is more than a word, document or an idea. It needs to be a way of life, something that eventually we do not have to consciously think about but that just *is*.

There have been some good efforts towards inclusive thinking in recent times. Evidence of disability issues appear in our popular soap operas (which have a huge effect on public thinking), workplaces have to make their buildings accessible and disability 'friendly', and schools are now directed to fully include children with special educational needs.

Dyspraxia is one of an increasing number of recognised hidden disabilities, and the fact that it is hidden brings with it a whole set of challenges and difficulties as children who look apparently 'normal' seem to be misbehaving or not trying to conform to 'normality'. In order to become truly inclusive there is a great deal of work to be done. However, by understanding the child with dyspraxia, the family and our own fears and reservations about a condition we do not really understand, we can take another step towards facilitating learning and improving our practice as more children with dyspraxia are recognised in our mainstream schools. A small percentage of children with dyspraxia will acquire a statement of special educational needs, the vast majority will not, and it is with these in mind that we will go on to explore some of the issues that we may not have considered in the past. These children learn differently but they *can* learn. Teachers have to know how to teach them in a way that will be effective for the child with dyspraxia as well as all the other children in their class.

Children who do not display behaviour that is considered 'normal' or who do not seem to understand what it is you are trying to impart can be anxiety-provoking. Yet, once you have met and worked with these children you can appreciate that they are not so different than any other child, and it is often extremely rewarding to be part of their success.

In order to be truly inclusive we need to see children with dyspraxia as part of a wider picture, which is filled with those children who learn in a recognised and accepted way and those who don't, alongside those who may need adaptations to the environment, differentiated work or specific medical care within the school day. The challenge is to accommodate all those children within a mainstream classroom and for that diversity of need to become accepted as 'normal'.

The largely negative history of special education and the way it has filtered into our culture is something we rarely think about on a conscious level, and yet it informs our behaviour. It is my belief as the mother of a young man with dyspraxia that in order to progress towards a truly inclusive society we all need to reflect on our own thoughts, ideas and practices. Without a huge attitude shift, people who have a disability will always remain on the outside looking in. Inclusion is more than an idea; it has to be a state of mind.

The teaching profession has undergone phenomenal change in recent years, and the demands on teachers to change, adjust, record and account are second to none. The barrage of reforms that teachers have been expected to accept in the last decade have in themselves been very anxiety-provoking and it is necessary to acknowledge the stresses in the system. It is also important to recognise that teachers are now expected to embrace inclusion almost without question and usually with no or very little training in special needs education. They are also exposed to the ever demanding issues of resource provision, the constraints of time, and the demands of the curriculum they deliver. It is no easy task, and the idea of learning about each child with a recognised special need in the classroom must be both overwhelming and exasperating, especially if a teacher has no real interest in special needs in the first place.

Teachers by the very nature of their profession feel that they have to do something with a child. Learning, literacy, citizenship and obedience are examples of the way in which a teacher aims to mould the child into the ideal of what he should be, or what society expects of him. Mainstream teachers on the whole are taught to teach children who learn 'normally'. That is, those children who follow an expected pattern of development and are the round pegs who fit neatly into the round holes. A child with additional needs may question the framework of the teacher's knowledge and experience. The square peg that challenges their expertise.

My concern in the field of education is that both teachers and pupils (able-bodied and those with a disability) have often been raised in an atmosphere and culture of negativity. The government is asking (or is it telling?) the mainstream education system to change. It emphasises social inclusion, that teachers should embrace diversity, focus on the individual and not the disability. These sentiments and actions are all very laudable but what I am suggesting is that until we can look to and challenge our own deep-rooted unconscious prejudices, assumptions and opinions, no amount of goodwill, good ideas, legislation, increased resources and training will change our practice or more importantly our desire to change our practice.

It is surely by finding some of the answers within ourselves that we can enable it to truly succeed.

Key points

- Difference is something that many people find frightening or unpleasant.
- We need to explore our own emotions before looking further.
- Teachers and other professionals can work more effectively if they explore their own prejudices.
- Government initiatives, without the support of those on the shopfloor, can have little impact.
- People with a disability such as dyspraxia should be *part* of society.

Chapter 6

Understanding parents

The concept of parent–teacher partnership is by no means new, but the current Code of Practice (2001) places great emphasis on its importance and contains a new chapter which is devoted to this area in which it recognises the need for cooperation if children with special educational needs are to meet their true potential.

Section 2:6 says:

> Positive attitudes to parents, user-friendly information and procedures and awareness of support needs are important. There should be no presumption about what parents can or cannot do to support their children's learning. Stereotypic views of parents are unhelpful and should be challenged. All teachers should bear in mind the pressures a parent may be under because of their children's needs.

There has been a great deal written about this area of educational need in recent years and yet in practice there often seems to be a lack of empathy from both sides, and the extremely important relationship between parent and teacher can so easily break down. This may be as a result of not truly understanding the position and perspective of the other party. Both parents and teachers are under a great deal of pressure in the current educational climate and this chapter attempts to offer some insight into those pressures and the impact of them.

Parents

> Mothers of children with problems carry a tremendous emotional burden. Few occupations carry as much and those that do carry a different kind. Fathers of neurologically handicapped children do not escape from the burden, but they carry it differently.
>
> Sometimes the weight of the problem seems too much to bear, and the presence or severity of the problem is denied in order to cope. Or parents recognize the severity and then they search and search for better answers to a difficult situation.
>
> (Ayres, 1979, p. 7)

Being told, or suspecting that your child has a special need is a devastating realisation, and families are very vulnerable at this time.

It is usually (but not always) the mother who deals with the day-to-day realities, the therapists, the schools, the 'how can I make this easier for him?', and they are usually in need of support for themselves at this time. This is support that they rarely receive from any professional means. It is important to realise that at this time, parents too have special needs.

Special needs and grief

Many people go through a period of grief. This may sound dramatic to some or perhaps simplistic, but is not so difficult to understand when you appreciate that this is a process brought about by loss.

When a child is diagnosed as having 'special needs' in a way the parents lose the child they thought they had. Many of the unspoken aspirations, dreams and plans they had are lost. Simple things like a family bike ride can no longer be taken for granted. The prospect of their child struggling to achieve the things others take for granted may bring about sadness and despair. Their future chances and prospects take on a different meaning. Other parents talk about university placements, travel plans and job prospects, while the parents of a child with special needs may have to reconsider these options. They become isolated from the normal conversations about development, achievement and future aspirations. Yes it is a loss, and it can leave individuals feeling very alone if they are struggling to come to terms with their emotions on their own.

Parents may feel:

- **Disbelief**: he'll grow out of it. Wait and see.
- **Anger**: why me? Why my child?
- **Guilt**: perhaps it was something I did. Should I be doing more?
- **Frustration**: no one believes me. What can I do?
- **Tearful**: emotionally labile. Coping one minute, crying the next.
- **Moody**: loss of temper more quickly or more often than usual.
- **Irrational**: unreasonable but uncontrollable behaviour.

Parents may feel some, or all of these things. They are coping with many confusing emotions, and it is helpful if those around them can recognise this. Mothers sometimes feel that their partners are adding to the considerable pressure they are already under, by not recognising their despair. The relationship with their partners can suffer on an emotional and physical basis, as people feel more and more alone in their grief. It should be remembered that mothers and fathers might not be in agreement about the child's difficulties or the approach that is being taken. It is wrong to assume that they will be present as a united front. The relationship between mothers and their children and fathers and their children is different and the expectations they have of their children may also be different.

Other children in the family can also suffer, as they are confused or unsettled by unusual undercurrents in the home.

Learning to cope

The first thing to try and acknowledge is that it is all right for a person to feel, however they are feeling. As individuals, we all have our own way of coping and of dealing with our grief. What one person experiences, and how they react may be very different from another's, but each is valid and important. If possible, it can be a huge relief for a person to try to share their feelings with someone close, or the kindred spirit of someone who has 'been there'.

As parents become more aware of their child's difficulties and needs, their emotions change, and often mothers experience a kind of chronic sorrow. The sadness never quite leaves but becomes tolerable to a greater or lesser degree, depending on the successes and/or failures of their child.

Children are sensitive to the moods and actions of their parents, and the last thing the parents really want is to cause any more suffering. However, this doesn't mean they need to, or should deny their own feelings and needs. Couples and families need to deal honestly and openly with how they are feeling. Another parent or a local support group may be a worthwhile contact in the initial stages of this period. The Dyspraxia Foundation has a number of regional support groups throughout the country and even if the idea of attending a support group is not very appealing, it may be helpful to just chat on the phone. Teachers should be able to direct parents to these support organisations. Family and friends can help too. They might not be able to find the right words to say, but could perhaps give the person in question a break, a hug or just 'be there'. It is all too easy to avoid someone if they are dealing with something to which you cannot really relate. Friends may feel guilty if they talk about their own child's successes and achievements and it may be tempting to avoid a mother who is experiencing the hardship of trying to come to terms with their own child's difficulties and differences. Sometimes it is enough for a friend or relative simply to acknowledge openly the struggle that parents often go through. It is easy to forget to acknowledge the relentless pressure those families are often subjected to. Perhaps other family members, and friends discuss this strain amongst themselves but do not like to discuss it with the person to whom it is happening.

It can be very isolating, being the parent of a child with dyspraxia, and sadly it is often a desperate struggle to get the child's needs recognised and addressed. It is an additional pressure that most families never experience and have little understanding of, but it can have devastating consequences and usually results in a change of family dynamics. Professionals need to be aware that the family is vulnerable and sensitive in the initial stages of coming to terms with their child's difficulties. They also need to be aware that suddenly the family is subjected to all manner of questioning and scrutiny in order to establish what is happening with their child, especially prior to a diagnosis actually being made. Children with dyspraxia are often grossly overassessed, as different people concentrate on fragments of the child rather than a multi-professional team assessing the child's needs and deciding what would be the best way forward. It is very hard to watch your child being assessed over and over again and to have little control of this. It is probably fair to suggest that everyone involved in the assessment and support of children with dyspraxia is well meaning, and some may feel threatened by the parents who at times are angry or simply desperate. Therapists and doctors can at times seem to treat the child as the next person on the waiting list. That one little person is extremely precious to the carer who is attending with them, and must be treated with the appropriate sensitivity and care.

It may be useful for professionals to consider the following when dealing with families:

- **Acknowledge their pain**. Never tell a parent that 'it could be worse'. Parents know that. They are not dealing with what could have been, but what *is*.
- **Don't tell parents you know how it feels**. You may well be sincere, but it simply is not true in the majority of cases.
- **Do treat parents as equals**. Parents often feel that their whole personalities have changed. They have to become assertive and tenacious and be able to spend vast amounts of time learning about policies and procedures of which they had no previous knowledge. Parents are and need to be seen as at least equal partners in the care and support of their child, and to be treated with respect and sensitivity.
- **Do remember that parents' priorities are just as important as yours are**. Lack of resources, or having to prioritise between children is just too painful to hear. Each child is important and deserves the best that is available.
- **Don't treat parents as though it is they who are disabled**. Parents often feel 'disabled by association'. They are advocates for their children.
- **Do allow parents to have bad days**. Parents can only cope wonderfully some of the time. They have bad days too, and on those days all they want is for the condition and all its trappings to go away, they wish they never had to go to another meeting in the role of 'competent parent'.
- **Don't have a conversation about the affected individual in his or her presence unless you involve the child in what is being said**. It is rude and demeaning. The individual is devalued enough and the parents may feel too battered to defend or assert themselves. It may well be that the parents are as guilty of this as anybody, but it is true to say that when families visit occupational therapists, paediatricians, etc. there is rarely a private area where the child's condition or needs can be discussed without the child being able to hear. It is as if when the child is given something to keep them occupied, they are thought to become deaf. Imagine being objectified enough that you become almost invisible to the people who are meant to be helping you.
- **Do recognise that parents have a right to be selective with advice**. Parents might not want to take your advice even if they have sought it! They usually do what they think is best for the child in the knowledge of all the influences that affect him or her.
- **Don't rush in to give assistance before you have ascertained that it is wanted**. People with disabilities and those caring for and supporting them are proud and protective. They, quite rightly, want to achieve by their own efforts and to relish the success. Taking things out of their hands, even with the best intentions, only adds to their frustration and lowers their self-worth.
- **Do try to be forgiving**. Parents of children with special needs often upset and alienate people in their desperation. Teachers and support assistants are familiar figures and often fall foul of the exasperation and frustration a parent is experiencing. Please try to remember what drives them, and that what they really want is your cooperation and involvement.

It is incredibly difficult for parents to watch their child struggle with almost every task they attempt to perform. It can be wonderful but is exhausting and truly draining to live with a child with dyspraxia full time. Having to prompt their every action, to think and act on their behalf, to anticipate what might happen in order to keep them safe and secure and to make a supreme effort to make all other children welcome in the hope that one of them will befriend the child the parents love. Parents of these children are rarely offered any respite, and they fear that their child will not be understood and supported appropriately in groups and activities and clubs, which are offered during school holidays. Indeed the behaviour of these children can be difficult to understand, a real puzzle that even their parents struggle to unravel.

It may be enough in the first instance for a parent's grief simply to be acknowledged. In an ideal world, access to counselling would be beneficial to very many parents who discover that their child's development is cause for concern. Any parent can empathise with another about the responsibilities, the hopes and desires, and the fact that our children are about the only thing for which we would lay down our lives. That makes parenting a very powerful issue and the pressures involved with it very great even in the best of circumstances. Additional pressure and strains are brought to bear on the parents and siblings of children with dyspraxia.

If other parents and teachers begin to empathise with these parents then a great deal of their pressure would be alleviated just by acknowledging that pressure. It is of course true that there are a minority of parents that do not want to acknowledge their child's dyspraxia and that makes life very difficult for the teachers dealing with that child. However, it is my belief that the majority of parents do want to understand and assist in their child's education.

Perhaps teachers, SENCO's (Special Educational Needs Coordinators), could make an initial appointment with parents to discuss their fears and to acknowledge their pain. Then regular meetings, which need not be too frequent, could be arranged to show a real interest in the parents' point of view and their contribution to their educational programmes. Making parents feel that their knowledge and skills are both recognised and appreciated goes a long way to alleviating the pressure felt by these families. Parents do have legal rights in the assessment and statementing process and so it is important that they are in full possession of all the information relating to their child. They should also know to whom they should turn for that advice, i.e. The SENCO (or perhaps she/he should be called the Inclusion officer).

Quotes from parents:

'I am feeling really wounded, like part of me has been damaged.'

'I was absolutely desperate for information.'

'If I wake up tomorrow and discover that this has all been a mistake, and that there isn't really anything wrong with him, I still will never be the same again.'

'I feel isolated.'

'It strikes me that my colleagues at work compare dyspraxia to a tangible illness from which recovery is rapid and complete.'

'I feel compelled to tell people . . . to excuse him.'

'I lost the child that I thought I had. I now have to re-evaluate all the things I took for granted. It's like grieving.'

'It's strange . . . one day you are rolling along as ever, the next day you wake up with a child who has special needs.'

'I fear for my child.'

Gill says:

I can remember being filled with dread when a teacher asked if I could spend 'just 10 minutes' with my son every evening in helping him with his letter and word recognition. You see my son was, at that time, seeing an occupational therapist, a speech and language therapist, an optometrist and a physiotherapist. I was having to take him out of school and take time off work to transport him to these appointments and eventually lost my job because I seemed to be forever going backwards and forwards to various appointments. Finances (and relationships) at home were a little strained. Each therapist had asked me to spend 'just 10 minutes' every evening with my son supporting his or her particular programme of activity. That was nearly an hour every evening with a child who was already exhausted and who didn't want to work with me anyway. I was his mum, not his therapist. There was tea to get for the other children and their homework to supervise, the dog to walk, the ironing, the cleaning . . .

I felt like screaming and each evening the therapy that I felt I had to do if I was to be a good mother became like a battleground. My child was disabled and if I didn't do what all these learned people asked I was failing him, so I made him do it. We completely forgot how to have fun, to laugh, to just enjoy each other. I will never forgive those well-meaning professionals for all that grief. It really took its toll.

Sheila says:

I can remember talking to my son's teacher about the fact that he was simply unable to follow the complex rules of the football or netball practice he was offered as his PE activity. He told me that he hated PE, but he was a really fit and active boy and I knew that appropriate PE activities would be really enjoyed by him. My son's occupational therapist backed up my information with a written report on perceptual skills and the importance of them for activities such as team games. The teacher was very sympathetic and said that he would look at some differentiated ball skills for my son, and I happily informed him that he was excused from the dreaded football and would be doing something that he enjoyed in PE that week. I arrived at school a little early to collect him the following day. It was PE out on the playing fields. I couldn't see Johnny and guessed he must be doing something different with his support assistant. And then I saw him, kitted up for football, a team colour blazoned on his shirt, expected to be a team player. He was attempting to hide behind a drainpipe and was talking to himself in a very animated way. He looked both lost and quite mad. I sat in the car and sobbed. I would never arrive early again; it was just too heart-breaking.

Angie says:

I had collected a drawer full of assessments relating to my son. The trouble was that my LEA [Local Education Authority] seemed reluctant to take the reports of professionals outside the area seriously. I seemed to need to have yet another aspect of his development assessed before any action could be taken. Clinical and educational psychologists, speech and language therapists, occupational therapists, a paediatrician, a behavioural optometrist, auditory technician, and various other 'necessary' people saw him. I remember someone coming to the door at home. She had a black bag and my little boy with dyspraxia assumed it must be another diagnostician and ran away. He was to be found huddled in the corner of the lounge, his face pale and his eyes anxious.

I looked at him and thought 'what have I done to this child?'

I would never let anyone put him or me through that again, but at the time I was desperately trying to get his needs recognised and someone always seemed to want more.

Jill says:

It was three years into the process of having my child with dyspraxia formally diagnosed and therapy put into place before anyone even asked how I was feeling. That person was an occupational therapist who had never met my child or me before and who was totally shocked when I seemingly overreacted by bursting into tears in response to a courteous enquiry. I had contained the grief, worry, frustration and had watched my child struggle for three years before anyone outwardly enquired as to what effect it was all having on me. I don't think that occupational therapist has any idea how much she helped me really, the relief was overwhelming.

Key points

- Acknowledge the parent's skills.
- Involve the parents in decision-making.
- Meet with the parents regularly.
- Direct them to a support group.
- Talk to the siblings if they seem to be suffering.
- Remember the child is about more than schooling and therapy.
- Share information sensitively and appropriately with peers and *all* other staff.

It is with the pressures on teachers and parents in mind, that we will go on to explore some areas of dyspraxia, which make access to the curriculum difficult. It is usual in our experience to find that when the child's needs are understood and catered for, the parents are relieved and buoyant which, in turn, makes the teacher's job both easier and greatly appreciated.

Any parent whose child has dyspraxia will empathise totally when I say that 'when Joe shines, so do I!'.

Chapter 7

Handwriting and dyspraxia

The most apparent symptom, which epitomises the combined difficulties experienced by children with dyspraxia, is in handwriting. Handwriting involves many complex processes, which are often assumed to develop spontaneously. Effective handwriting requires a child to have proficient cognitive, perceptual and motor abilities in order to record knowledge, thoughts and ideas physically onto paper. However, the profound impact of perceptual and motor dysfunction on the child with dyspraxia has an enormous influence on the child's ability to write legibly, fluently and at speed. It is inevitable that this frequently required activity becomes a source of considerable effort and distress to many children throughout their school careers.

In today's society with the advances in computer technology the need to write seems to be ever decreasing. Letter writing has been superseded by instant connections across the globe via e-mail, note taking can involve the use of Dictaphones and other recording devices and even the need to write shopping lists has been minimised with the introduction of online shopping. As a university student many years ago, I recall writing spurious notes afraid that I may miss some crucial piece of information which I might require for the next assignment or examination. Today students are offered lecture notes online, linked to supportive websites, and have very little need to record any notes at all.

Unfortunately, despite the reduced need to write in adulthood, handwriting is still used as the main means of recording information in schools today. It is also the primary method for assessing a child's understanding and knowledge. A large percentage of the child's school day involves writing-related activities, be this in literacy, maths, topic work, science, history or geography. The need to write increases during Key Stages 3 and 4 with the additional requirement that the child learns to write at speed, therefore it would seem appropriate that the early development of handwriting is well taught with a consistent style and method being adopted. Sadly this is not the case. Very few teachers during their initial training were taught how to teach handwriting; therefore early handwriting instruction is based on personal experiences of handwriting instruction. In many cases this involves a mixture of styles according to the ethos of the day. For example in the period between 1970 and the introduction of the National Curriculum a variety of models were adopted from Barnard, Gourdie, Jarman, Nelson and Marion Richardson. The use of italic was also in vogue influenced by calligraphers such as Wood, Yates-Smith and Blunt, followed by emergent writing where children were encouraged to experiment with letter forms and make marks which had meaning for himself (Sassoon, 1999). This resulted in children enjoying an eclectic mix of styles, which they were able to experiment with. However, for those children who struggle with this multifaceted task, inconsistencies in style and tuition serve to amplify their difficulties.

The need to introduce handwriting clearly from the start is supported by the fact that many children enter full-time education having spent considerable time writing perhaps no more than the letters of their name. The National Curriculum gives specific guidelines on its expectations regarding handwriting. However, it does not offer suggestions relating to achieving these objectives. It is assumed that by the age of 9, the majority of children will have mastered handwriting skills and have developed a fast, fluent, legible hand, which enables them to record, at speed, a considerable range of information. Children with dyspraxia know that in reality this is not the case, and that many handwriting problems are just beginning to emerge at this age when pressure increases to write in a cursive style, both fluently and fast.

Each school is required to have a handwriting policy, a detailed programme to follow which is consistently applied throughout the child's time in that school. The programme should be reflected in teachers' writing styles and handwriting lessons. Sadly, handwriting tuition often takes a back seat under the increasing demands of the National Curriculum.

Children with dyspraxia particularly struggle with that which the National Curriculum describes as secretarial skills, rather than compositional concerns. Most children with dyspraxia *know* what they want to put down on paper but the physical application of handwriting limits their ability to do so, consequently these children's ideas and stories, and ultimately their knowledge base is not heard. In a relatively recent study Addy (1996b) investigated the learning styles of children with and without dyspraxia. A group of twenty-five children with dyspraxia aged 9 to 11 years were asked to comment on the subjects they were involved with at school. Each child unanimously stated that school consisted of three subjects: writing, art and PE. In addition, each reiterated 'I am rubbish at all of these subjects'. By comparison their peers talked about the variety of subjects available to them at school, these included geography, aspects of maths, algebra, fractions, geometry, history, biology and the considerable variety of learning experiences they had available to them. These were discussed rationally in relation to the individual talents, abilities, interests and ambitions. Handwriting is a huge issue for these children and one that can dent a child's confidence very quickly.

The handwriting difficulties experienced by children with dyspraxia are far-reaching and typically will present as follows:

- Poor pencil grip.
- Abnormal posture.
- Awkward position of paper to the child.
- Inaccurate hand–eye coordination.
- Incorrect letter formation.
- Incomplete letter formation.
- Erratic sizing of letter forms.
- Mixture of upper- and lower-case letters.
- Poor alignment of writing on the page.

- Lack of consistency in direction of ascenders and descenders.
- Inconsistent spacing between words, either no spaces, too narrow or too wide.
- Heavy or light pressure through the pencil.

The sample below is typical of a child with dyspraxia.

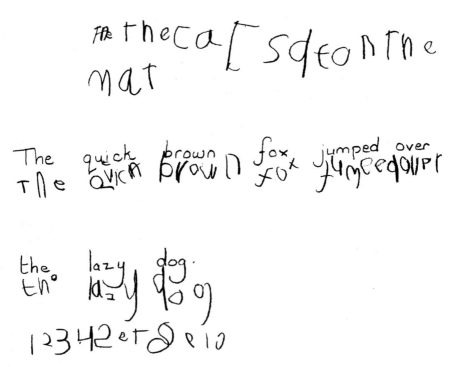

Figure 7.1 Sample of handwriting from a child aged 7

It is therefore important that we attempt to address each of the above difficulties in order to provide some possible solutions.

Posture and positioning

First, in order to control the intricate movements required by the upper limbs and hands in particular, it is important that the child is positioned correctly. This is especially important as many children with dyspraxia struggle to sit still and this is exacerbated when the furniture used is inappropriate for the child. In today's classroom we have a range of bright practical furniture suited to the average child. Unfortunately many children do not fit into this 'normal' standard. Ideally a child should have a seat which places his hips, knees and feet at 90°. Tables should be at the height of the child's elbows when flexed (bent). This will provide the child with a secure base from which to work. If the child is too short for the chair, either foot blocks need to be used, to provide a platform from which to work, alternately old telephone directories serve as useful foot raisers. If the chair is too low, this needs to be adjusted or a higher table and chair introduced to the classroom.

The position of the paper in relation to the child is also important. This should be at an angle in alignment with the angle of the arm, be this left or right. Some children with dyspraxia will place the page square onto the table. This causes the arm to press against the side of the body, which causes writing to become compacted and restricts the fluency of writing. It is important to be aware that some children are doing this to reduce their position in space. These children may be, what we call, tactile defensive. Children who are tactile defensive are oversensitive to touch and therefore may avoid any physical contact from others. To avoid the possibility of being touched, the child ensures that his personal space is very narrow. Children who are tactile defensive can also be identified by their discomfort when wearing certain materials, for example woollen jumpers might make them feel too itchy. Close proximity with others, for example standing in queues might be particularly uncomfortable. If this appears to be the case, the child should be allowed more space, and given a seat where no one sits in close proximity. The position of paper can be highlighted using a paper locator. This is a large sheet of A2-sized card which has a template of paper position and resting hand position inscribed on it.

Laterality

Once the position and posture of the child has been addressed, it is important to address the pencil grip. Before looking at the actual position of the hand on the pencil, it is important to clarify the child's hand dominance. Hand preference can often be observed before the age of 2 (McCartney and Hepper, 1999). However many children take longer to develop a true preference; only establishing a distinct inclination by 7 years of age, and some stay ambidextrous throughout their lives. Delayed hand dominance is typical in many children with dyspraxia. Of the population, 90 per cent is right-side dominant, while 8 to 10 per cent are left. However, 30 per cent of left handers have bilateral representation or mixed dominance. This is demonstrated in mixed laterality having for example a left-eye dominance, right ear, left hand and right foot. Children with mixed dominance, which can often be seen in children with dyspraxia, tend to appear uncoordinated and there is increased concern that those with confused dominance are more at risk from developing dyscalculia (mathematical disorder), as well as having dysgraphia (difficulties in handwriting and auditory–visual-processing disorders (Haseltine, 1999). There is some evidence that difficulty at birth or premature birth may delay preferential hand use and increase probability of confused laterality (Leiderman and Coryell, 1982). It is important to note that confused laterality does not cause a specific learning difficulty such as dyslexia or dyspraxia; rather it may be an additional symptom.

As many children with dyspraxia take an unusually long time to establish laterality, they may continue to swap a pencil grip from right to left hand for many years. This can leave the teacher very confused about which hand they should encourage for writing tasks. The advice that follows may help to define the preferred hand.

Provide the child with a double-sided blackboard or easel (Figure 7.2). Position the child at the edge of the board so that he cannot see either side. Give the child a piece of chalk in both hands. Initially lead the child through a series of prewriting patterns such as loops, waves, etc.

Figure 7.2 Activity to determine hand dominance

Encourage the child to repeat these patterns, independently, three times each day for a period of one week; each practice session should take approximately 10 minutes. By the end of the week examine the patterns and try to ascertain which has the most consistent and fluent style. If this is the pattern on the right side encourage use of the right hand for writing. If it is the pattern on the left side encourage the use of the left hand for writing.

Pencil grip

Once a preferred hand has been identified, it is important that the child adopts a correct pencil grasp. A typical pencil grip uses a three-fingered tripod grip. This allows the child to see the point of the pencil clearly and locate direction. Many children with dyspraxia hold their pencils awkwardly. Often this is due to the anxiety of having to write, but some grips have a more strategic purpose. Many children will roll their thumb over the shaft of the pencil so that the pencil is held in the web space of the thumb. This position ensures that the pencil is held very tightly but restricts fluency of writing strokes. Similarly many children roll both the thumb and index finger over the shaft of the pencil so that a very tight grip is used. This grip is often used by children who have poor tactile sensation, and is common in children with dyspraxia; in order to gain as much sensory feedback as possible, the pencil is gripped so that the maximum skin surface area is utilised. Children who have poor joint position sense also use it as they are not receiving accurate information from their joints and muscles regarding the fine muscle responses required to write effectively. The tighter the grip, the greater the feedback.

One of the ways to address this difficulty is to address the source, in other words to improve proprioceptive feedback; this can be done using many in-hand manipulation tasks, which improve dexterity. Examples can be found in programmes such as Handprints: Home Program for Hand Skills, and Tools for Teachers™ (see appendix for details).

Alternately pencils, which position the fingers in an appropriate arrangement can be helpful, triangular pencil barrels, and triangular pencil grips are readily available, as are many pens with bevelled rubber finger placers, these are effective as they afford a better grasp. An alternative grip can be used whereby the pencil is placed on the upper part of the hand between the index and middle fingers. This is effective in reducing direct tip-of-finger pressure.

If the child's fingers appear to be 'floppy' and joints seem very mobile this can indicate a problem known as hypotonia (low tone). A tight grip may be used to simply maintain the pencil's position in the absence of regulated muscle tone, in this case adapted pencils such as Handhuggers, Grippit 2000 and ring pens can all be useful (see appendix for suppliers). In addition it is possible to simulate accurate muscle tone using strategically placed material plasters over the child's finger joints. Strips of plaster are placed on extended (straight) index and middle fingers, as well as the thumb, to cover all joints. When the digits are bent to hold the pencil, tension is experienced which supports the fingers and provides additional proprioceptive feedback and tactile sensation through the hand.

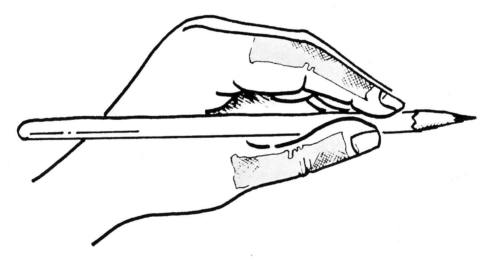

Figure 7.3 Simulation of increased muscle tone in the fingers and thumb involved in holding a pencil

The rule of thumb when considering a child's pencil position is that if a grip is used which enables the child to write fast, is effective and is not causing any physical pain to the hand, no matter how bizarre the grip, leave it alone! If the grip seems to be causing some discomfort, which can be observed by the child shaking his hand to relieve cramps, supporting his wrist or rubbing a sweaty palm, it is worth trying to correct it.

Pressure through the pencil

The next concern is application of pressure through the writing instrument. It is more common for children with dyspraxia to press down too heavily through the pencil, but some have the opposite problem of not pressing down hard enough. If we consider why this might be the case, it is possible to address this issue. We have described earlier how many children with dyspraxia have proprioceptive problems due to the dampened sensors located in muscle, tendons and joints as to the exact position of the limb in space, this effects coordination and in particular pressure of placement. To address this we need to try to improve the child's proprioceptive sense in his upper limbs. This can be done through a series of physical exercises that stimulate the receptors in the upper limbs. These can include the following tasks taken from the Speed-Up Handwriting Programme (Addy, 2004) which uses a kinaesthetic approach to address handwriting difficulties.

- Arm spirals. Hold the arms out in a horizontal direction, rotate arms starting with small spirals, these should increase, and then change direction gradually reducing in size again. Attempt 5 of these.
- Wall press-ups. Stand approx. 0.75 m away from the wall with arms at shoulder height touching the wall; attempt 10 press-ups so that the nose touches the wall.
- Ladies press-ups. Attempt 10 press-ups where it is not necessary to lift the stomach at the same time as the trunk.
- Bandage-gather (horizontal). Lie a crepe bandage in a horizontal position on a table. Place the wrist down on the table at one end; gather the bandage with thumb only.
- Bandage-gather (vertical). Lie the bandage in a vertical position. Place wrist down at lower end and attempt to gather bandage – using fingers only.
- Sit on a chair with hands holding each side, attempt to lift bottom off chair by pushing through straight arms, do this ten times.

These exercises will enhance the child's upper limb awareness by stimulating the prioprioceptors for approximately 40 minutes after which the response appears to 'dampen' until further exercises are used.

To further help the child to adjust pressure through the writing instrument, use a light-up pen available from many stationers. If the child has a tendency to apply too much pressure, they should be encouraged to write without triggering the light, if the child is unable to apply enough pressure they should be encouraged to press down enough to keep the light on. Strategies which use self-monitoring devices are very successful at effecting change.

In addition, carbon paper can be useful. Several sheets of paper are used with a piece of carbon paper between each one. The child who applies too much pressure is encouraged to write so that his script only shows through two sheets rather than four or five, the child who struggles to apply pressure is encouraged to press through to several of the carbon sheets.

If a child is struggling to apply pressure through the pencil, this could be due to the wrist position; it is therefore important that the wrist is positioned on the desk or kept in a lowered position. To ensure this, an angled board can be provided; this can be bought commercially or simply made from plywood. The angle should be between 25 to 30° depending on the child's needs. As an alternative, weighted wrist bands could be used to encourage placement of the wrist on the table, these should not be gym wrist weights but are straps or bracelets which can be piped with haberdashery or fishing weights.

Another solution to the problem of not enough pressure is to lower the height of the table being used. This is the only situation where lowered table height is appropriate. By dropping the height so that it is approximately 6 to 10 centimetres below elbow height, the child is encouraged to use the weight of the body to produce pressure through the writing instrument.

Hand–eye coordination

The perceptual components of handwriting also need to be addressed. Often we expect children to write before they have successfully achieved hand–eye co-ordination. This can be demonstrated when observing a child placing 2 centimetre cube bricks on top of one another. Many children with dyspraxia cannot achieve the placement of even four bricks without knocking them down. This is due to pressure of placement and significantly affects control of writing. If a child cannot place his pencil on an exact point, help will be needed before the child can progress onto the greater complexities of handwriting.

In this situation work is needed to develop proprioception and build up the shoulder girdle stability. This can be achieved using games which apply weight through the upper limbs such as; crab football, wheelbarrow traces, crawling activities, etc. In addition the child will need specific fine motor activities to promote accurate placement such as peg board placement, bead threading and commercially available games such as Kerplunk™, Buckaroo!, Jenga, Lego, K'nex to name a few. To ascertain how a child is progressing, place an A2 sheet of paper on a table and sprinkle it with sweets such as M & Ms™, Skittles™ or Smarties™. Ask the child to use his index finger to locate directly certain coloured or specifically located sweets. If they are able, they are rewarded. Later produce a sheet covered in coloured spots, provide the child with finger-paint and ask if he can place an index finger on the exact points. Reduce the size of this so that gradually you request that the child can place his pencil on an exact spot. Once achieved other aspects of handwriting can be tackled.

Form constancy in handwriting

Recognition and reproduction of shapes or forms are a fundamental part of hand-writing; therefore it is essential that we have adequate form constancy. This not only enables us to identify and distinguish shapes but also to differentiate between sizes of objects. It is this area of dysfunction that influences the child's letter formation and size. It is therefore important to ascertain whether a child can reproduce a series of shapes both from memory and from a copy. If these are distorted, then letter formation is likely to be affected.

The child would then need to spend some time using multi-sensory techniques to appreciate the qualities and dimensions of a variety of forms. For example sorting objects according to size, drawing round the body to appreciate proportion, creating various shapes in a tactile medium such as sand, salt, shaving foam and slime. Using therapeutic putty (which is available in a variety of densities, hence requiring differing amounts of pressure to mould and shape) or play doh to create various letter shapes. The child needs to be able to form simple shapes and lines before they can combine these to develop effective letterforms. For example they need to be able to produce a horizontal and vertical line, a circle, a square and a triangle. The majority of children with dyspraxia will find reproducing a triangle very difficult. This will also present in an inability to draw an x or y with correct alignment. This is because a diagonal line requires the child to cross two planes; left to right and top to bottom. You will observe that letters involving diagonals are usually the last to develop; therefore activities encouraging this plane-crossing are very useful. For example hand-clapping games in pairs where the hands cross to the opposite side of the body, geoboards, peg board patterns and spatial copying activities such as those demonstrated below all help to accommodate this difficulty.

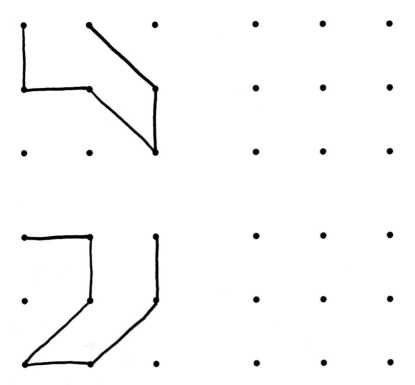

Figure 7.4 Spatial copying exercise

To help the child to develop an awareness of letter sizes, lined paper should be encouraged as far as possible ideally with clear reference lines to identify the central line, with a line above to indicate heights of ascending letters, and a line below to indicate descenders. As children with dyspraxia benefit from multi-sensory activities it can be additionally useful to use 'stop and go' paper which has a raised or bevelled line to help the child remember which key line they are working to.

Movement control

Once the child has mastered the reproduction of simple shapes, they are then ready to link these to letterforms and learn how each form can join with the next shape. To produce clear forms the child must realise that every shape or letter has a precise beginning and end. Many children with dyspraxia have what is commonly described as an overflow of movements. They seem to fidget constantly or shuffle from leg to leg when trying to stand still. These movements may be exaggerated when the child is excited or agitated and can be extremely irritating to teachers and parents alike. It can be seen overtly in PE when a teacher asks the group to run around the room in a certain direction. If the command 'stop' is called the majority of children will stop immediately, the child with dyspraxia, because of poor organisation will run on a few paces. This overflow of movements can also be seen in the child's handwriting, with many letters seeming to have no definitive starting and concluding point. For example:

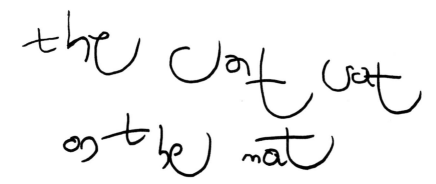

Figure 7.5 Illustration of letter overflow

It is therefore very important that the child appreciates that every form and letter has a specific starting place and finishing point. The *Write from the Start: A Perceptual-Motor Approach to Handwriting* programme (Teodorescu and Addy, 1996) suggests the following activity to address this issue.

A coloured reference point is given at the left side of the page with a different coloured point at the opposite side, in between are a number of reference points to guide the child from left to right. The lines vary in length and initially the child might overshoot the final point, but with practice success is quickly achieved. As the child progresses through the exercises, the reference points decrease and the child must predict how to track from left to right.

Early attempt	● ·●
Improved control seen with maximum reference points	● · · · · · · · · · · · · · · · · · ·●
Later attempts with fewer reference points	● · · · · · · ●
Final challenge	● ●

Activities relating to the production of shape along with those relating to starting and stopping will help the child to develop the precise control needed to form clear, legible letters.

Figure–ground discrimination and its impact on writing

We described in Part I of the book how many children with dyspraxia struggle to observe a figure from a background. This is also evident when the child is writing. When a line of words is written and the second line commences, the child becomes distracted by the previous line. This affects the alignment of writing on the page with a tendency towards lines merging together.

This again reinforces the need to use lines as a reference. Some children will need additional help using multi-coloured lines to guide them, being encouraged to write on, for example, a yellow line, followed by a blue line, then a green line, etc. as the child progresses, he will have less need to use such a variety of colours. Alternately a sentence cover could be used, as each line is written it is covered with the strip so that the child is not distracted by previous information.

Orientation and reversals

A further concern of those working with children with dyspraxia is the number of letter reversals. The letters f/t, b/d, p/d, n/u, p/q and m/w are frequently inverted. Other letter orientations are also erratic with the letters s, g and j being reversed. Often the child struggles to orientate letters appropriately and can be seen to 'rock' to and fro over the upper surface of the letter before a decision is made as to the correct direction. There are several ways to help children with orientation:

- Group letters and introduce the formation of these according to direction, i.e. clockwise or anti-clockwise. Therefore letters which require a clockwise orientation would be b, h, j, m, n, p, r, and those incorporating an anti-clockwise motion would be a, c, d, e, f, o, q, t, u, v, w, three letters require both orientations, g, s, and y.
- Provide puzzles where the child must select which item is inverted or reversed as in the example below.

- Practise letter forms using a kinaesthetic approach, for example practise writing letters in the air, initially guiding the child so that he can mentally visualise the letter orientation.

- Use odd-one-out puzzle books to encourage the child to observe the difference in objects.
- Encourage cursive writing from an early age; if a child is taught to join letters from the conception of handwriting, orientation difficulties will be dramatically reduced.

Spacing between words

The most common feature of handwriting, which is typical in children with dyspraxia, is poor spacing of letters and words. This often renders script illegible.

Typically if a child has gross motor coordination difficulties which affect his spatial planning, that child will inevitably have poor spatial organisation when undertaking fine motor tasks such as handwriting. The following scenario occurred recently at a local primary school.

On visiting a school one day, I noticed a group of Year 2 children who were having a PE lesson. On this occasion they were allowed the apparatus and were having a wonderful time. However, in one corner of the room a queue was beginning to form behind a 1.5 metre high gym horse. The group of children waiting were growing increasingly impatient as a lone figure struggled to manoeuvre himself over the horse to the mat at the other side. Shouts of 'get a move on' and 'hurry up' had no effect on the little boy who was desperate to find out a safe way of getting down from the horse, the agitation from his peers simply added to his anxiety. The teacher looked on in exasperation and was surprised when I quietly said to her 'I bet he doesn't leave any spaces between his words when he writes?'. She turned in astonishment and asked 'How do you know that?', rushed to the classroom and returned with a book where his writing demonstrated no spaces. This boy had obvious spatial assessment difficulties. He was evidently struggling with the perceived height of the gym horse, so it was inevitable that poor spatial organisation would also impact on other aspects of his life.

This example not only indicates how spatial difficulties impact on both fine and gross motor coordination, but demonstrates how, by addressing spatial dimensions using a variety of methods, the results can have far-reaching consequences in many childhood activities.

To address spatial difficulties simple games can be used such as:

- 'How many steps?': standing with the child, ask 'how many steps will it take you to reach that chair?'. The child then guesses. They are then encouraged to take those steps and monitor their own movement. Initially the child may grossly under or overestimate the distance, but with time the estimations gradually become more accurate.
- Obstacle courses: these can incorporate the child being blindfolded and being guided around a series of obstacles by a partner, or the child pretending to be a

robot and only following the precise instructions of a robot mechanic situated at the opposite end of the room.

- Puzzle book mazes can help with spatial planning.
- Grid exercises.
- Block-cube building can also help a child to judge space as the success of construction is dependent upon adequate spatial positioning.
- Peg board patterns can also help in organisation of space.
- Specific activities relating to handwriting can be implemented. The most important being the early introduction to cursive (joined) writing. Children who have been taught to join lettering from Key Stage 1 have considerably fewer visuo-spatial errors than those who are introduced to this style in Key Stage 2.
- Graphic activities such as those incorporated into the *Write from the Start: A Perceptual-Motor Approach to Handwriting* programme (Teodorescu and Addy, 1996).
- Physical activities, which link whole body movement to handwriting tasks such as those incorporated into the Callirobics™ programme can also help.
- The use of grid paper can offer a guide so those children can be prompted to leave a space between each word.
- Similarly by encouraging a finger space between words, legibility improves.
- Patterning with fragmented lines can help the child to learn about flow and when to break a pattern to move the arm across the page as illustrated in Figure 7.6.

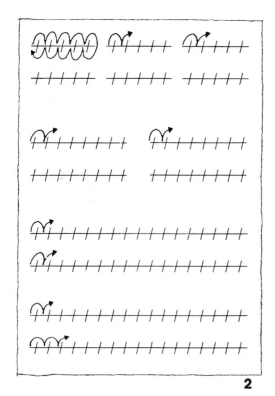

2

Figure 7.6 Activity to help develop fluency. (Taken from *Write from the Start* programme, LDA Ltd)

Fluency

When a child is introduced to handwriting in the UK, they are encouraged to produce pre-writing patterns during the Foundation Curriculum, this is then halted as letter formation is taught; each letter being taught individually during Key Stage 1, then joining re-emerges during Key Stage 2. There is considerable evidence that this interim stage is unnecessary and can limit fluency of handwriting (Laszlo and Bairstow, 1983, 1984, 1985; Sassoon, 1990). During Key Stage 1 it is possible that many children produce clear legible letters with orientation in opposition to the norm. These frequently practised, but seldom corrected letters will cause difficulties when the child begins to join letters to produce cursive handwriting. It is at this time that fluency and subsequently speed deteriorates.

Sassoon (1999) reiterates this:

> If older children try to develop a joined writing for themselves from a base of poorly formed and spaced print script, the result is often unsatisfactory. This is why an integral exit stroke on the first letters that children learn is so vital, and one of the reasons print script has fallen out of favour, despite the fact that many still perceive it as easy to teach.
>
> (1999, p. 111)

To prevent this from happening it is important to introduce cursive writing from the onset. The child can experiment with prewriting patterns, be introduced to letter formation with joins, but then must be shown how the letter will fit into the context of the word.

Fluency and speed can also deteriorate as the child comes under increasing pressure to increase written output within an allocated time. This problem is one that many children with dyspraxia face as they approach Key Stage 3. Organisation and motor difficulties impede the child's output. The child is expected to simultaneously compose and produce writing while contending with poor motor coordination, erratic organisation and complex perceptual processing.

To help the child we have to enable him to write spontaneously. At this age practice and rehearsal of letterforms are not sufficient to change style and improve fluency, a different approach is required; one which helps the child to develop a mental image of the letter forms and how they connect. A kinaesthetic approach is successful in this instance. This involves the use of many multi-sensory techniques that stimulate the child's appreciation of letter form without the reliance on vision. Techniques include writing on chalkboards, patterning to music, drawing in sand or salt, use of clay or dough. Specific writing programmes can also help to develop fluency such as the Speed-Up programme, Handwriting without Tears™ Take Time and Callirobics.™

Speed can be a significant issue when the child is faced with examinations and it is at this stage that teachers may need to consider whether the child is eligible for extra time, use of a word processor or allocated a scribe. The Joint Forum for GCSE and GCE (1999) provides guidelines regarding eligibility of extra assistance.

Augmentative technology

There may come a point in time when the child's handwriting is seriously affecting his learning and is having a detrimental effect on the child's self-esteem and confidence. At this point alternatives to writing must be considered. This commonly occurs around the age of 8 years. A variety of technology is available and each child must be assessed individually. Handwriting for Windows™ is a nice alternative if children want to word-process information but print it out so that it looks like script. The Fairley House Touch Typing Programme is a comprehensive programme as is the Read and Type a Gift for Life scheme (Mayhew, 1997). Organisations such as Abilitynet and The Writing and Computers Association can provide impartial constructive advice on appropriate software and hardware.

In concluding this section on handwriting, it is important to revisit issues regarding the volume of handwriting children with dyspraxia are expected to produce (given that as adults we don't need to write very much at all) and for teachers to accept the challenge to answer the following questions:

- Are there alternatives to writing which help children to express what they know?
- Can alternatives be considered?
- Can technology be used more practically in the classroom? Could other media be used to present children's work, i.e. video recordings, comic books with pictures taken from magazines, multiple choice quizzes, Dictaphone recordings, drama presentations, and so on.

We live in a world where children read less and watch more; surely children with dyspraxia can use their creative talents to enable teachers to appreciate their knowledge base without the need for copious writing.

Chapter 8

Dyspraxia and mathematics

With the introduction of the National Numeracy Strategy (DfEE, 1999) concerns are increasingly expressed regarding the mathematical ability of children with dyspraxia. Therefore, there is a need to clarify the precise needs of children with dyspraxia in respect to this subject.

Difficulties with maths are a common concern expressed by parents, teachers and children alike. However, there may be several reasons why children struggle with maths which has nothing to do with dyspraxia as a condition:

- It may be that the child has a poor self-image of himself as a mathematician. It is almost acceptable to confess to 'being poor at maths', yet it would be embarrassing to express a similar attitude towards reading. Maths is often regarded as a subject for which you either have or have not a talent.
- The child may struggle to understand the methods taught by the teacher. While this could be an excuse afforded to many subjects it is mostly applied to the teaching of maths. If you ask a group of adults which teacher they struggled to understand at school, the reply is commonly 'the maths teacher'. The problem being that the language, rules and procedures of maths are complex. The teacher really needs to be in tune with the needs of each child and how the children process information. It is in this subject more than any other that the learning styles adopted by both teacher and child need to be compatible.

Saracho (1997) states that potential difficulties arise when teachers' own cognitive style is at variance with that of the pupils. For example, the tendency of teachers to rely on paper-and-pencil computation exclusively to the neglect of hands-on types of activities can have a negative effect on students' learning (Hughes *et al.*, 1997). This needs to be recognised in the design of the learning tasks, the presentation of materials and in support that teachers offer.

To identify the learning styles adopted by children who struggle with mathematics either the Test of Cognitive Style (Chinn and Ashcroft, 1993), the Learning Combination Inventory (Johnston, 1996) or *Learning Styles* by Vail (1993) can be used to identify individuals' preferred method/s of working.

- It could be that there might be a lack of mathematical experiences at home.
- Different cultural backgrounds can also influence a child's ability in math. This was experienced firsthand as recounted below.

Alydda was from Bangladesh and was experiencing a number of difficulties at school due to her poor motor coordination and perceptual processing. One of her difficulties was arithmetic and in particular laying out calculations correctly so that accurate computation could be achieved. As I addressed this issue within the school environment I was visited by her parents who informed me that she was to return to Bangladesh in the future for an arranged marriage, and that I should focus my therapeutic involvement on domestic tasks. I assured her parents that her future responsibilities would require her to work out the domestic budgeting and that certain mathematical skills would be important. We were allowed to continue to help Alydda provided that the material covered in maths was based on real-life problem-solving issues, which required critical thinking.

- The language of maths is unique and as such can be extremely complex for children with perceptuo-motor or literacy difficulties, for example the word 'add' can also be expressed as 'plus' or '+'. There are very few other subjects where there are so many descriptions for a single action.
- Gender differences also can influence an individual's perception of mathematical ability, with the historic assumption that boys are better at maths than girls. There is no substance in this, but this fallacy still influences children's confidence (Arnott *et al.*, 1998).
- Children with dyslexia will have problems with maths, specifically the language of math, sequencing, orientation and memory, e.g. learning tables, formulas, etc.

Many children with dyspraxia will also have specific difficulties with the processing of mathematics and you may hear the term 'dyscalculia' used to describe their difficulties. Some believe that this term is unique to children with dyslexia, but this is not the case. Developmental dyscalculia or 'mathematical disorder' (American Psychiatric Association, 1994) is a cognitive disorder of childhood affecting the ability of an otherwise intelligent child to learn arithmetic. The term developmental dyscalculia is applied to children whose arithmetical ages are definitely below average in relation to their mental ages (Kosc, 1974; Sears, 1986; Maeland and Sovik 1993). The difficulties that such children have may involve many different skills. These skills normally develop between the ages of 4 and 7 years. Presentation is usually in the early school years.

There are numerous types of dyscalculia identified by Kosc (1974) and Sharma and Loveless (1986). Some of these are more evident in children with dyspraxia. Some of the terms used appear quite technical but are important in describing the various types.

1   Spatial dyscalculia. This refers to difficulties in mathematical understanding as a result of difficulties in visuo-spatial assessment and organisation. This is the most common form in children with dyspraxia. Specifically the following problems are noted:

(a) erratic placement of the digits, especially when undertaking subtraction and addition;

(b) inability to estimate or approximate numbers;

(c) inability to judge spatial dimensions;

(d) difficulties understanding three-dimensional figures;

(e) difficulties translating two-dimensional figures into three-dimensional figures;

(f) digits and figures can often be reversed or inverted (therefore 9 may be written as 6);

(g) confusion over whether a procedure should be tackled in a horizontal or vertical direction.

2   Anarithmetria. This involves confusion with arithmetic procedures such as mixing addition, subtraction, multiplication, and other written operations. The disorganisation in planning actions typically associated with dyspraxia interferes with the interpretation of mathematical procedures in the child with dyspraxia.

3   Lexical dyscalculia (or alexia). The language of maths is extremely complicated and as such it is easy to muddle or confuse terminology. It is particularly hard to translate a procedural word into its associated symbol. Therefore confusion can arise when, for example, translating the symbol + into the word addition and vice-versa.

4   Graphic dyscalculia (or agraphia). This is a disorder in the ability to write the appropriate symbols and digits required for calculations. As dysgraphia (difficulty writing) is a key feature in children with dyspraxia, it is inevitable that writing numbers will also prove problematic.

5   Practognostic dyscalculia. This describes impairment in the ability to manipulate concrete or graphically illustrated objects. The word practognostic literally can be translated as 'pract', which arises from the word practical or hands-on and 'gnostic' meaning knowledge; therefore this form of dyscalculia involves a difficulty in practically applying mathematical knowledge or procedures. According to Senzer (2001) children with practognostic dyscalculia may not be able to arrange objects in order by size, compare two items based on their respective sizes, or state when two objects have identical size and weight.

Dyscalculia is never seen as an isolated specific learning disorder, it is often associated with abnormalities of either the right or left hemisphere of the brain. In children with dyspraxia it is predominantly the right hemisphere of the brain which is affected and difficulties include visuo-spatial deficits, tactile perception and psychomotor ability (Rourke and Conway, 1997). Montis (2000) also noted imbalanced posture to add to the list of features.

If we look briefly at areas primarily responsible for perceptual processing we can see how this connection has been made.

Right-hemisphere dysfunction

• Profound inability to conceptualise number quantity – this presents in an inability to estimate amounts.

- Constructional dyspraxia – poor organisation of mathematical procedures.
- Poor development of visual spatial and motor skills.
- Sensory inattention.

Dyscalculia generally is more *marked* in left-hemisphere lesions which are why it is frequently associated with difficulty in reading and writing (dyslexia).

However, in children with dyspraxia the difficulties experienced are very specific and as such it is important to identify exactly where the child's difficulties lie and the reasons and potential solutions or activities which may address the concerns.

Does the child understand spatial concepts?

In mathematics there are numerous terms used to describe position in space, some of these are subtly different, others use many words to describe the same location, for example: beside, next to, by, all describe a similar location. Under and below are also similar, as are adjacent and opposite. It is also necessary that the child develops strategies for remembering right and left in order to help with work on symmetry. It is important that all terms are understood before mathematical procedures are introduced. To help a child to acquire these terms introduce the following games/activities:

- 'Simon Says' incorporating spatial terms. For example, Simon says stand next to the table; Simon says sit under the poster, etc.
- Spatial card games available from LDA Literacy Kit (see appendix). Create an obstacle course and place positional terms near the obstacles to indicate which direction you want the child to move in. For example 'under' the table, 'over' the chair, 'by' the rope.
- Play the game 'port and starboard' but alter terms. For example start at the central position looking midline, shout right or left, the children need to run to either the left or right side of the room, commands such as 'scrub the floor' = lying on the floor, 'up the stairs' = child pretends to walk up stairs. Additional requests can be used according to the child's needs and the whole class can be involved.
- Encourage awareness of inverted or reversed objects through the use of visual discrimination puzzles such as 'Let's Look' (LDA Ltd).
- For younger children, provide a doll's house or garage. Make up a story about a family who lives in the house encouraging the child to move figures around the building, and incorporate positional terms.
- Create the memory game pairs but each pair is made up of a positional term, i.e. 'under' and a matching pictorial representation of an object placed under a selected item.

Can the child recognise mathematical symbols?

It is important to check that each child recognises and understands the symbols involved in mathematics. Often mathematical problems are presented in a problem-solving manner and the translation of these into symbols and figures becomes complex and confusing. It is not only important that they recognise that a ÷ means division, but also that words such as add, plus, take away, can be represented by symbols.

For example:

Mark has 7 sweets, Jemma has 5. How many sweets do they have altogether?

Presented either $7 + 5 = 12$ or

$$
\begin{array}{r}
7 + \\
5 \\
\hline
12 \\
\hline
\end{array}
$$

James had 6 Beyblades, and then he gave 5 to Alex, How many does John have left?

$6 - 5 = 1$ or

$$
\begin{array}{r}
6 - \\
5 \\
\hline
1 \\
\hline
\end{array}
$$

To help to develop these concepts create the following games:

* Memory game: this is based on the common childhood game of pairs (pell-menism) where a child must turn over two cards and find matching pairs. The person with the most pairs is the winner.

  Game 1 Make up a series of cards containing two of each of the following mathematical symbols, i.e. + □ × ÷.
  Game 2 Make up a series of cards but for each symbol pair it with the associated word, i.e. ÷ and divide.
  Game 3 Make up a series of cards but provide all terms and symbols connected to each procedure, i.e. add /plus/ +. Share/ divide/ ÷.

* With the same cards described above, play 'snap'.
* Henderson (1998) suggests that many children prefer diagrammatic or pictorial explanations of symbols.
* Colour-code symbols to differentiate between each, especially those which look similar such as + and ×.

Can the child recognise numbers when presented in various forms?

Not only can procedural concepts change in maths but also the presentation of numbers. Therefore a child will need to recognise that the terms two and 2 mean the same thing. To help develop these skills:

- Make up number pellmenism cards which incorporate different ways of defining number concepts i.e. four/4/, nine/ 9.
- Create a number and symbol lotto game.
- Adapt a game of dominoes by placing a sticker over *one* end of each domino, which states the number of dots, in this way the child has to appreciate the number of dots and connect with the written number.

Figure 8.1 Adapted dominoes

- Use pattern cards or mosaic pictures to ascertain whether the child can define the various forms used to make up the picture.
- Create number patterns from mosaics, collages, balsawood or clay such as Fymo or play dough.
- Create cards, which have raised number shapes created using thick string and PVA glue. Blindfold child and try to guess the number.

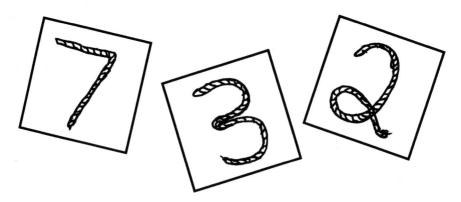

Figure 8.2 Tactile numbers

- Direct the child to creating numbers in a variety of mediums such as salt, flour and shaving foam.
- Write numbers in the air or on the child's back: can they recognise these?

Can the child write the numbers and symbols needed for calculations?

It is important not only to recognise digits and symbols, but also to be able to write down the symbols accurately as this will affect calculations. As previously mentioned, many children with dyspraxia struggle to reproduce diagonal lines due to an inability to transfer across two planes, top to bottom and left to right, this can be accepted to a certain extent, when writing letters, but can have devastating consequences in calculation when x is translated into +.

In addition, it is also common for children to transpose certain numbers; therefore 24 may become 42 which will again significantly affect the calculation. In order to address these difficulties implement the following strategies:

- Provide a number and symbol stamper kit so that symbols do not need to be written at all (available from Early Learning Centre).
- Practise spatial exercises, which include diagonal lines to encourage crossing over dimensional planes.
- Trace numbers in sand, salt and foam or dough. Alternately write numbers using a thick pen on coarse sandpaper to maximise kinaesthetic feedback.
- Teach the writing of numerals in groups where numerals (3 and 5) and (6 and 9) do not occur in the same groups, i.e. 1, 2, 3 making sure that 3 is formed correctly before introducing 4, 5, 6 and making sure that 6 is correctly formed before introducing 7, 8, 9 and 10 (El-Naggar, 1996).
- Help to develop the shape of numbers by using number stencils.
- Encourage orientation of number forms using 'Rol 'n' Write' numerals (available from LDA Ltd).

Can the child form the shapes needed in geometry?

Difficulties in the perceptual area of form constancy will affect the child's ability to reproduce shapes, especially those which contain a diagonal such as a triangle or diamond. Shapes produced will appear distorted which will worsen if drawn from memory without a visual cue. Three-dimensional drawings will be exceptionally problematic due to the child's inability to reproduce shapes and measure depth. Children with form constancy problems will also struggle to differentiate size and therefore may not see the subtle differences in many objects.

To help with this:

- Use multi-sensory activities which develop an appreciation of form such as 'I draw a shape upon your back. Guess the shape'.
- Create shapes, numerals and symbols in the air with eyes closed to help child develop a mental image of the various forms.
- Use stencils to create shapes.
- Use gummed paper shapes to create patterns and forms.
- Introduce a range of posting boxes with three-dimensional shapes (do not publicly use those designed for a considerably younger child).
- Play games, which involve visual discrimination such as odd-man-out.
- Copy simple designs.

- Play the washing game: Buy a series of small clothes and string up two washing lines. Make a series of paper garments (two each) and peg a series of clothes on one line.

    (a) Ask the child to create a matching row with the other clothes.
    (b) Ask child to order the clothes according to size small at one end and larger items at the other.
    (c) Create a sequence of clothes on one line and ask the child to copy the sequence

    As an alternative use real clothes on a real clothesline.
- Create a series of cards with pictures of various sizes. Ask child to order these according to size.
- Provide a selection of cups containing several items, i.e. 5 buttons, 2 pegs, 5 beads, 6 cubes, ask child to arrange in size order placing the cup with the fewest items at one end and the one with the most at the other. Ask questions relating to the groups, i.e. which cup has more items than the cup with the buttons.
- Use stacking toys to differentiate size variations such as stacking cups, Russian Dolls, Interlocking barrels, etc.
- Involve the whole class in a sorting activity. Ask the children to order themselves across the classroom according to size. Do the same but use other measurements such as feet size, hair length and hand size.
- Use 'Geoboards' (Happy Puzzle Co.) to create shapes and patterns.
- Introduce three-dimensional forms, using 'Activities for Geometric Solids' (LDA Ltd) to guide the child towards appreciating three-dimensional qualities.
- Play a game called 'Cuts', take a shape such as a triangle and cut off each corner; discuss what is remaining. 4 triangles? Do the same with other forms.
- Put a variety of three-dimensional shapes into a bag or box: can the child identify the shape by touch alone?
- Play a game called 'describe the shape'. Provide a series of shapes or a series of connected shapes. Describe these to a partner who has to identify the shapes involved. For example, it has three sides and the base is horizontal.
- Play 'guess the shape'. Each person creates a simple model from Lego or Duplo, which is then hidden from the view of a partner. The partner must try to replicate the shape by asking a series of questions, which can only be answered 'yes' or 'no'. That is, 'do I start with a red 8?'. 'Yes.' The winner is the person who can reproduce the model within twenty questions.

Does the child place calculations erratically on the page?

If a child has spatial organisation difficulties, they will struggle with place value, copying from the board, book or work card, identify spatial denominators, represent three-dimensional figures in two dimensions, and recognise two-dimensional objects in a given solid.

Spiers (1987) in his classification system for calculation errors, described 'spatial dyscalculia' involving the improper arrangement of numbers during computation. This is probably the most significant problem experienced by children with dyspraxia.

To help:

- Use squared paper, locating each digit or symbol in one square.
- Provide a line of direction (ideally in colour) for calculation either left to right (horizontal calculations) or top to bottom, right to left calculations.
- Reproduce calculations encouraging spatial planning through the use of similarity; therefore write all hundreds in one colour, tens in another and units in a further colour. When digits are placed in columns, the child will be attracted to similar colours and this will help the child to scan in the appropriate direction.
- Space the calculations on a card arranging these so that they will be scanned according to the proximity to each other. An arrow can be added to help focus direction. For example:

```
3     5     6      ⇩
1     4     2  +
5     3     8
_____

_____
```

Alternatively:

⇨ $6 + 2 + 1 =$

$5 + 1 + 3 =$

- Teach hundreds, tens and units by creating coloured columns writing all hundreds in one, tens in another and units in a further coloured column.
- Practise alignment using the game 'Connect 4' or 'Four in a Row' to encourage child with accurate placement of counters to form a line vertically, horizontally or diagonally.

Can the child estimate amounts?

One of the earliest spontaneous uses of quantity concepts is the judgement that one group of objects contains more than another, this is based on relative size and density. It is essential for a child to be able to determine whether something has more or less in terms of quantity prior to the calculation of exact amounts. This requires an ability to estimate amounts. Estimation is important not only in school but also throughout life and requires adequate spatial organisation. The following strategies can be used to develop approximation.

- Guess the number. In partners, a number is selected by a child who writes this down (for example the number 6), his partner must now guess the number by asking a series of questions. Only the answer 'yes' or 'no' can be used in reply. For example 'is it more than five?'. 'Yes.' 'Is it less than eight?' 'Yes.' 'Is the number seven?' 'No.' 'Is the answer six?' 'Yes.' Increase complexity by escalating number size.

- How many steps. Stand along side child and select an object in the room. Ask the child to guess how many steps he thinks it will take to reach the object. Following the guess, the child can then attempt to count the steps towards the object.
- Large as life (adapted from Edwards *et al.*, 1993). This game encourages problems to be broken down into smaller components. Real-life examples can help to add meaning to the estimations. Start with a simple question such as 'How old are you?', progress onto 'How many months do you think that is [calculate this]?', 'How many days old do you think that is?' 'How many hours old are you?'

    Alternately: how many bricks were used to build a wall?

    How many words on a page of a book?

    How many legs does a cow have? How many legs do ten cows have?
- In a small class group, give the child a bag of sweets, say that they are going to share them out equally between all members of the group, ask the child if they can guess how many sweets each person might get? Deal the sweets out and demonstrate how this is known as division. Were there any left in the bag? Continue to teach division using estimation of real-life events.

Does the child struggle to maintain his place when following a visual procedure?

One-to-one matching of words and objects being counted is also a fundamental skill from which basic mathematics is grounded. This can be affected by poor figure–ground discrimination distracting the child from the systematic marking of each object and hence establishing one-to-one correspondence when counting.

A difficulty in pointing to selected items in an organised manner also impedes the linking of numbers to components. This could be effected by hand–eye coordination, lack of attention and/or poor figure–ground discrimination.

In addition many of our present-day maths books are well presented in terms of pupil interest having coloured pictures interspersed with logic and reasoning problems. These may be stimulating to the child without difficulties, but for the child with dyscalculia difficulties may occur because of an overload on the child's visual senses. The following suggestions can assist.

- Written information is restricted, sums are taken (either the page is cut up, or photocopied) and each sum presented one at a time, thus reducing overload.
- Use a marking-off strategy, physically marking off amounts when counting.
- Use sorting activities such as Rainbow People by Eichild or Creepy Crawlers by LDA Ltd. Introduce puzzle books such as the *Usborne Puzzle* series, i.e. Puzzle Castle, or use 'Where's Wally' puzzle books for the older child, where a specific item is hidden on each page.
- Highlight key procedural words with an underliner or highlighter pen.
- Encourage the child to underline the mathematical symbol being used.
- Check estimations with a calculator.
- Ensure that the font size on worksheets is large enough.
- Avoid elaborate computer programs.

- Create a game similar to a word search but with numbers rather than letters. See if the child can find a certain number among the grid. Start with a twenty-five square grid and progress up to a one hundred square grid.
- Painting by numbers will help children to match a number coded colour with its respective part on the picture.
- Play bingo, starting with a few numbers and progressing to a full card.

Does the child struggle with sequences?

Sequential memory difficulties are more common in children with dyslexia than dyspraxia, but the poor organisation skills of children with dyspraxia can interfere with the retention of sequences and therefore help is needed to address this:

- Provide a sheet of random numbers. Join the numbers in the correct sequence from one to ten.
- As an alternative ask child to join all the even (odd) numbers in sequence.
- Grade a variety of dot-to-dot activities carefully graduating complexity.
- Limit the amount of instructions.
- Repeat instructions while at the same time providing a written prompt.
- Sequencing games can be useful for over learning, i.e. adapted version of 'Mrs Brown went to town and bought . . . four bananas', etc.
- Give a sequence of numbers but miss out one. Can the child identify the missing numeral? Increase and grade complexity.
- Escalator: create a drawing of a high-rise block of flats with approximately twenty floors. The person in the escalator wants to go to the fifteenth floor. Children take it in turns to throw the dice, which elevates the person to the selected floor number, if the number goes beyond the home; the next throw makes the elevator descend. The winner is the first person who can make the elevator land on the home floor (adapted from Edwards *et al.*, 1993).
- Learn multiplication through rhymes and song. Use timestable squares (Chinn and Ashcroft, 1993, p. 57).

Does the child struggle to understand fractions?

Children with dyspraxia often have a perceptual difficulty known as visual closure (see Chapter 2). Difficulties in this area affect object recognition, completion of jigsaw puzzles and in relation to maths, the understanding of fractions. It is therefore very important that multi-sensory activities are used to help with this:

- A variety of textured mediums can be used to demonstrate proportions physically such as creating cakes from play dough, which can be divided into half or quarters.
- Use fraction dominoes (LDA Ltd): children match the simple written fraction to the fraction diagram.
- Introduce Fraction Lotto (LDA Ltd): this may need to be adapted initially so that only four fractions are addressed initially before progressing onto the nine-part board.

- Use actual objects such as a cake; physically demonstrate fractions by dividing items. Alternately use 'Pizza Party' (LDA Ltd) which provides a series of mock pizzas to be divided according to everyone's 'taste'.
- Fraction Stax™ (LDA Ltd): a variety of pieces can be placed on a peg to appreciate fractions.
- Take a piece of paper and fold it according to the fraction being taught, i.e. half, quarters, etc.

Does the child struggle to follow concepts of weight and measures?

Children with dyspraxia have poor proprioception (knowing where their limbs are without the need for sight) and therefore struggle to appreciate volume and weight, as the muscle receptors are not as acute as in other children. To accommodate this it is necessary to provide practical ways of measuring weight and velocity using instrumentation and measures. For example use Funtastic Frogs,™ bucket balance, and number balance scales.

Does the child have an understanding of time?

Time is such an abstract concept, that it is small wonder many children with dyspraxia struggle with this essential skill. Not only do children have to master digital time but also analogue and the numbers involved are far from easy to calculate. We have sixty seconds in each minute, sixty minutes in each hour and twenty-four hours in each day separated into two twelve-hour periods! In addition to working with number bases: twelve, twenty-four and sixty, time-telling also requires an understanding of fractions and the ability to count forwards and backwards using a circular number line. Many children with dyspraxia require literal explanations of time; for example, the concept of tomorrow may be described in terms of one sleep and two meals; lunch and dinner.

In order to help a child learn time, try the following activities:

- Introduce the child to specific times, which have some significance to the child, i.e. the time that school starts and finishes, break time, lunch time, etc. Demonstrate how the various times are presented on the clock. Demonstrate the differences between each time span, i.e. show how school starts at nine o'clock and lunch is at twelve noon; therefore to calculate the time you can take nine away from twelve to see that there are three hours between these periods. Later the half-hour position can be introduced, so that if school commences at nine o'clock and break time is at half past ten, there are one and a half hours between these periods.
- Link both the analogue clock and digital clock to times of certain favourite TV shows, demonstrating how the time is written.
- Introduce Time Dominoes (LDA Ltd): these dominoes provide both analogue and digital time displays.
- Time Snap (LDA Ltd): this game of snap has both analogue and digital clock faces on rather than dots.
- Help child to estimate time by asking them to select a task that they estimate

could take three minutes, i.e. walk round the schoolyard. Introduce child to the words they will need to know with respect to time, i.e. annual – once a year, month – approximately four weeks, one year – twelve months, etc. (Henderson, 1998).

- Use rhymes and raps to remember seasons and months of the year, i.e. thirty days have September, April, June and November . . .
- Demonstrate how the year is split into quarters in a similar way to the analogue clock, each quarter represents three months and one season. Compare the sections with the clock.
- To encourage children to read digital time, create a game of pairs using digital examples which are paired with the interpretation in words, i.e. 10.20 = 20 minutes past ten, 15.30 = half past three.
- Create a similar game to that described above but compare the digital time to those presented on an analogue clock face.

Does the child struggle to manipulate practical maths materials physically?

Motor skills are not only vital for recording responses to mathematical questions but are also involved in the problem-solving process. Initially there are two main strategies adopted in order to help a child to count both requiring considerable manual dexterity:

- Counting-all strategy. The use of fingers to count, i.e. 3 + 4 = three fingers are counted, then four fingers then both are added together beginning at one and ending at the answer seven.
- Counting-on-using the example of the same sum the child raises three fingers and adds on four more counting upwards from 3, 4, 5, 6, 7.
  Geary (1990) suggests that the use of strategies which reduce demands on working memory resources, such as counting on fingers, should be encouraged rather than suppressed.

In addition much of the apparatus needed in mathematics requires considerable dexterity. Manipulation of Cuisenaire rods, money, rulers and protractors all require good bilateral skills and adequate judgement of pressure through the apparatus. Children with dyspraxia commonly have difficulties in these areas and simple adaptive solutions are the key to success.

- Place a blob of Blu-tack on the ends of ruler to stabilise when drawing lines, alternately use My First Ruler™ (LDA Ltd) which has a comfortable handle attached to make ruling lines easy.
- Use a calculator with large keys. Customise calculator with colour-coded stickers so that the × and + are not pressed in error.
- Use lacing cards to develop manipulation skills and progress to using lacing multiplication cards.
- Encourage sequencing skills and dexterity by giving children a sequence of colours to follow while threading buttons onto a lace.

- Provide a pegboard pattern template and ask pupils to create a simple pattern using the template. Their friends then need to follow the template using either jumbo grip pegs or beaded pegs. It is possible to start with a twenty-five-hole board and progress to a one-hundred-hole board.
- Customise board games by gluing thick string along the tracks and adding dividers made from pieces of straw with PVA glue, so that the child appreciates the distinction between each square or place.

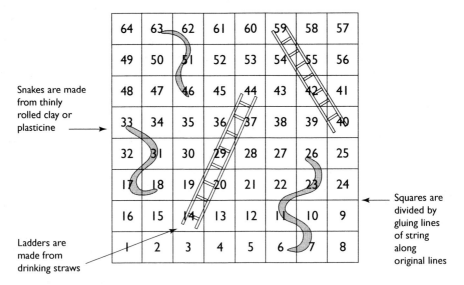

Figure 8.3 Adapted board game

- In the playground use a ladder as a number line to help with spatial organisation when adding or subtracting. Physically take the child over each rung counting as you do so.

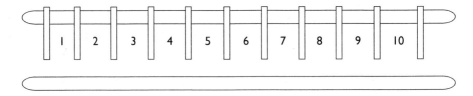

As the child progresses, smaller number lines can be provided with lines between being partitioned using segments of coloured drinking straws attached with PVA glue.

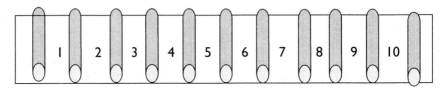

Does the child struggle to maintain concentration and attention?

Children with poor dexterity and visual perception may find the very thought of maths lessons overwhelming. The prospect of manipulating, sequencing, organising and learning new concepts at the same time as following specific procedures can cause considerable stress and anxiety. At the same time the volume of material presented may simply cause the child to 'switch off'. Behaviour may deteriorate as a way of opting out of a potentially negative experience. It is very important that the child is given information piece by piece, and the child governs the pace of tuition. Above all it is essential that the teacher is sensitive to the motivation, attention and concentration of the child and has utilised a variety of multi-sensory techniques to reinforce new procedures. In order to maintain the child's attention and motivation:

- Ensure that work is of an age-appropriate level.
- Revisit previous work/skills to reinforce previously introduced concepts but use novel ways of reinforcing procedures.
- Do not rehash previously completed work.
- Give time – individualise programmes.
- Give the child scrap paper to experiment with procedures and practise certain methods.
- Observe how the child works through a calculation to identify his learning style. Chinn and Ashcroft (1993) identify two key learning styles adopted by the majority of children and describe them as 'inchworms' and 'grasshoppers'. An inchworm is unable to see the whole problem and focuses on procedural detail. The grasshopper, on the other hand, will leap through procedures to reach a solution, without being able to see how it was accomplished. Inchworms follow through formula in a prescriptive manner, grasshoppers are intuitive, tend to estimate, form concepts and explore solutions. The authors suggest that teachers must be aware of these two styles in order to accommodate the different learning needs of each child.
- Don't expect the child to complete the same amount of work as the rest of the class during the numeracy hour, and certainly don't penalise the child by withdrawing 'choosing or free time' because he hasn't produced as much work as others have.
- Don't be surprised if you need to go over and over the same procedure time and time again.
- Don't expect the child to concentrate if the environment is noisy.
- Spend time looking at the work needing to be tackled, through the eyes of the child and consider how it might be best adapted to suit his specific needs.
- Be very patient.
- Remember that there is a need for overlearning but beware of 'motivational burnout'!

It is hoped that by identifying the specific difficulties that children with dyspraxia have with mathematics, and by explaining the reasons why these occur, that it is possible to modify and adapt the curriculum in order to address them. The suggestions provided are few and there are many practical books, which provide further resources for teachers to address the complex nature of dyscalculia (Edwards *et al.*, 1993; Henderson, 1998; Chinn, 1998; Yeo, 2002).

Chapter 9

Inclusive physical education

> Luke rushed into our after-school motor skills group exploding 'Mrs Addy, Mrs Addy guess what's happened? Something amazing has happened!'. His enthusiasm was infectious. 'You'll never guess what!' he said again. 'I am on the school football team!' Knowing 9-year-old Luke's passion for football and how much he struggled with motor coordination, this was a tremendous accolade. 'Wow!' we all said, sharing his enthusiasm, 'what position are you going to play in?'. 'Oh, I don't have a position as such, I am the manager!' he replied. 'Wow! That is brilliant' we replied, 'what will it involve? Will you have to choose the team'?. He shook his head. 'Will you have to work out tactical manoeuvres?' 'No' he said. 'Will you have to coach the guys and keep them motivated?', he shook his head again. The group was obviously running out of ideas at this point and so we said 'well, what *is* your role as team manager? What will you have to do?'. 'Well' he said 'I have to stand at the pitch side, and yell as loudly as I can for my team'. I tried to suppress my dismay at the role he had been given, but remained positive. At the end of the session Luke quietly took my hand and said 'You know, although I know it's important to be the manager, I'd rather be on the team and score a goal!'.

This story is typical of the experience of many children with dyspraxia. Unfortunately we still live in a society where sporting prowess is admired and physical ability is graded according to giftedness, ability or clumsiness. For a child with significant coordination problems it is often difficult to select activities which will guarantee success and which are not demeaning to the child. It is also difficult to select team activities in which the child will not 'let down' his peers and subsequently be ostracised for failure to perform adequately.

For the child with dyspraxia, physical education is an area of the curriculum where the extent of the child's difficulties is most apparent and may be clearly observed. This is because within the classroom the child is in a predominantly stationary environment whereas a physical education lesson involves a child-moving environment (Piek and Edwards, 1997).

The goal of physical education is to 'help develop motor competence and confidence in the physical and social self'. In addition it contributes to problem-solving skills, develops interpersonal skills and forges links between the school and community (Sugden, 1991).

Most children, especially at Key Stage 1, have a natural enthusiasm for movement and it is keeping them still which can be a problem for many parents. However, the child with dyspraxia may have many fears regarding movement especially within large gym halls, due to poor spatial organisation and inadequate coordination. Teachers may struggle to know how best to help the child without jeopardising the other children in the class.

Many children with dyspraxia may be being seen by an occupational therapist or physiotherapist outside school, where gross and fine-motor coordination are addressed. On occasions, when possible, the therapist will liaise with the child's teacher but is not really seen as part of that child's educational team. What we would like to suggest is that in order to assist fully the child with dyspraxia, therapy and education should come together, so that the child's motor needs are addressed in the school environment and are reinforced during playtime and after school. In order to do this, therapists *must* understand the attainment targets of the National Curriculum, and in turn teachers would benefit from understanding therapeutic aims and objectives based on the child's physical and perceptual development. This collaboration can help the child to have his needs addressed on a regular, consistent basis, without the need to be withdrawn from the school environment. The following tables are examples of how the National Curriculum (Department for Education and Employment, 1999) objectives at Key Stage 1 can be adjoined to the therapeutic goals of paediatric occupational therapists and physiotherapists. The left-hand column highlights aspects of the National Curriculum programme of study; the right-hand column suggests the skills which are required to achieve these goals from a therapeutic perspective. By comparing these we can see that both teachers and therapists are aiming for similar targets.

National Curriculum recommendations

Key Stage I

AGE 5–7 YEAR GROUP 1–2

Attainment target   Level I

Pupils copy, repeat and explore simple skills and actions with basic control and coordination. They start to link these skills and actions in ways that suit the activities. They describe and comment on their own and others' actions. They talk about how to exercise safely, and how their bodies feel during an activity.

1   Acquiring and developing skills

Curriculum   *Therapists*

Pupils should be taught to	Skills required
(a) Explore basic skills, actions and ideas with increasing understanding. (b) Remember to repeat simple skills and actions with increasing control and coordination.	• Basic motor skills • Motor planning • Motor organisation • Sequential planning

2   Selecting and applying skills, tactics and compositional ideas

Pupils should be taught to	Skills required
(a) Explore how to choose and apply skills and actions in sequence and in combination. (b) Vary the way they perform skills by using simple tactics and movement phrases. (c) Apply rules and conventions for different activities.	• Sequential memory • Motor planning • Organisational skills • Flexibility of ideas • Short- and long-term memory

3   Evaluating and improving performance

Pupils should be taught to	Skills required
(a) Describe what they have done. (b) Observe, describe and copy what others have done. (c) Use what they have learned to improve the quality and control of their work.	• Expressive language • Good observational skills • Self-awareness • Self-monitoring skills

4   Knowledge and understanding of fitness and health

Pupils should be taught	Skills required
(a) How important it is to be active. (b) To recognise and describe how their bodies feel during different activities.	• Body awareness • Self-confidence • Sensory feedback

5   Breadth of study: pupils should be taught the knowledge, skills and understanding through dance activities, games and gymnastic activities

6   Dance

Pupils should be taught to	Skills required
(a) Use movement imaginatively, responding to stimuli, including music, and performing basic skills (for example travelling, being still, making a shape, jumping, turning and gesturing.	• A sense of rhythm, balance, coordination, vestibular integration, spatial awareness, position in space, intact body schema, sense of body rhythm, controlled movement.
(b) Change the rhythm, speed level and direction of their movements.	• Controlled speed of movement encouraging vestibular integration and orientation.
(c) Create and perform dances using simple movement patterns including those from different times and cultures.	• Sequential movement patterns
(d) Express and communicate ideas and feelings.	• Imagination, understanding of feelings of self and others, understanding of rhythm, vestibular integration, form constancy, spatial concepts, spatial awareness

7   Games

Pupils should be taught to	Skills required
(a) Travel with, send and receive a ball and other equipment in different ways.	• Controlled movement, ability to start/stop and change speed of movement. Hand–eye coordination, foot–eye coordination, ability to judge space and form constancy.
(b) Develop these skills for simple net, striking/fielding and invasion-type games.	• Work in cooperation with others, spatial organisation, controlled hand–eye coordination, targeting skills, assessment of speed.
(c) Play simple, competitive net, striking/fielding and invasion-type games that they and others have made, using simple tactics for attacking and defending.	• Controlled motion, understanding of spatial concepts, spatial awareness, and figure–ground discrimination. Appreciation of rules and boundaries.

8   Gymnastic ability

Pupils should be taught to	Skills required
(a) Perform basic skills in travelling, being still, finding space and using it safely, both on the floor and using apparatus.	• Awareness of position in space, balance, motor coordination, spatial awareness, ideomotor processing.
(b) Develop the range of their skills and actions (for example, balancing, taking off and landing, turning and rolling).	• Motor control, proprioceptive feedback, projection, orientation.
(c) Choose and link skills and actions in short movement phrases.	• Sequencing, short-term memory, motor planning, spatial organisation.
(d) Create and perform short, linked sequences that show a clear beginning, middle and end and have contrasts in direction, level and speed.	• Sequencing, orientation, velocity of movement.

There is no statutory time allocated within the National Curriculum for the amount of PE taught each week, although the government recommends approximately two hours per week. This does *not* have to be taught in PE and will include extra-curricular activities such as football practice, gym groups, etc. The average school has approximately one hour to 90 minutes of PE each week. This allows school flexibility to allocate more teaching hours to other core and foundation subjects. Back in 1999, when the numeracy hour was implemented, in addition to the already-established literacy hour, the BBC News Online network expressed concern that the introduction of *core* subjects (literacy, numeracy and science) were influencing the amount of time spent doing physical exercise to the extent that the emphasis on the 3Rs was creating a nation of 'couch potatoes' (BBC News Online 21 August 1999). The *Guardian* 4 September 2002 reiterated this concern stating that 'primary schools have roughly halved the amount of time allocated to PE over the past five years or so, and only a third of children in Secondary Schools get two hours a week of PE compared with forty-six per cent in 1994'. It can be argued that children have access to a wide range of physical activities outside school, however many of these are costly, oversubscribed, and often not appropriate or suitable for children with motor coordination and perceptual difficulties such as those experienced by children with dyspraxia. Therefore it is very important that the physical education taught in schools is not only regular, but also appropriate to the child's needs. It is also essential that this is a positive learning experience whereby children have fun, achieve success and want to continue outside the school environment.

Most PE programmes adopted in schools are based around the QCA and DfEE (2000) *Scheme of Work*. These are relevant and useful to most children. However, many children with dyspraxia struggle with the expectations of some of this scheme and quickly become fearful of failure. Those children who are seen by an occupational therapist or physiotherapist for their difficulties may undertake additional physical activities. Suggestions from these therapy groups are given to school with the suggestion that certain activities are reinforced within school PE lessons as often as possible. Despite good intentions it is often impossible for the teacher to find time to administer consistently what seems like a series of activities over and above those stipulated in the National Curriculum.

One way to address this concern is to create a programme which will combine therapeutic activities and address the requirements of the National Curriculum. A collaborative programme will not only address the needs of the child with dyspraxia but can challenge the physical needs of the whole class. In this way the child with dyspraxia will undertake activities appropriate for his needs at least three times each week. This can only be beneficial, as we know that skills can only be improved and generalised with frequent practice in a number of different contexts.

The following programme is one example of how therapists and teachers can work together to develop motor coordination within the school PE curriculum.

It is written for children at the latter part of Key Stage 1 and can be adapted in complexity for children in Key Stage 2.

The ten-session programme covers a period of half a term and assumes that PE is undertaken once or twice each week in forty five-minute sessions. The sessions can be divided into shorter sessions if required. An equipment list is provided so that teachers can prepare for the lesson, well in advance. It also includes specific aims and objectives which will not only benefit the child with dyspraxia but all children in the class. The games incorporated are not necessarily those seen in typical PE lessons but are physically beneficial, meet the National Curriculum Physical Education agenda and are good fun!

Lesson 1

Aim: to develop hip and shoulder girdle stability, addressing sections 1–4 and 8a, 8b, 8c and 8d of Key Stage 1 National Curriculum PE programme of study.

Objectives

- to encourage weight-bearing through shoulder and hip girdles;
- to develop upper and lower limb girdle stability;
- to encourage proprioceptive awareness especially at the shoulders and hips.

1 Warm up by running around the room according to the teacher's instructions; forwards, backwards, sideways.
2 Run around the room according to the teacher's instructions; slow or fast.
3 Place two rows of mats on the floor across the room. Follow the leader to crawl across the room on the mats.
4 Keep the mats in place; divide into small teams and have a crawling race across the room.

5 Play 'follow the leader' across the room while in the high-kneeling position.
6 Change the teams. Have a high-knee walking race.
7 Each child takes a football. In the crawling position crawl across the room while pushing the ball gently and carefully with one hand. Speed is not important.
8 Create new teams and have a race pushing the ball while crawling.
9 Conclude with a game of crawling football.
10 Review the lesson by asking children which was the hardest aspect of the session. Did they think the lesson was physically beneficial?

Equipment required for session:

• numerous floor mats;
• footballs;
• four cones to act as goal posts.

Lesson 2

Aims: to further develop shoulder and hip girdle stability addressing sections 1–4 and 7a, 7b, 8a, 8b, and 8c of Key Stage 1 National Curriculum PE programme of study.

Objectives

• to further develop hip and shoulder stability but emphasising shoulder stability;
• to strengthen the shoulder girdle to develop coordination and consequently improve fine-motor coordination;
• to encourage balance and postural control.

1 Discuss the aims of the session to develop strength in the shoulders and hips which will help with handwriting, and balance. Review previous session's activities by discussing which activities needed the most control.
2 This activity assumes that the floor is wooded or is suitably polished. Provide a series of blankets or large towels, in threes, one child sits on the edge of the blanket, while the other two take hold of a corner each and pulls them across the room. No jerky movements are allowed. Change passengers.
3 Place a passenger on the blanket and ask them to close their eyes, their 'chauffeurs' must glide them around the room as gently as possible weaving and curving across the hall. Change passengers.
4 Have a race with other trios in the class to see who can pull the child across the room the fastest.
5 Children sit in pairs on the floor in the centre of the room. Children are positioned back to back; try to push each other across the room using feet only. Bottoms must remain on the floor at all times.
6 As above but this time feet should be together and legs straight, the effort to push his partner should come from the upper limbs hence utilising the shoulder girdle.

7   Individuals maintain a crab position and try to kick a ball between two low goals.

Figure 9.1 Position for crab football

8   Have a team game of crab football. It is preferable if only six children play on each side each game. The children must remain in the crab position and try to kick the ball into a goal; the team who score the first goal are the winners. Children with dyspraxia will tire very quickly in this game, so place in a position of defence and allow those in defence to sit on the floor when they need a rest.

9   Review session by discussing which part of the body had to make the most effort during the session, ask children whether their arms ached. Why might this be a useful activity?

Equipment needed for the session

- four cones to act as goalposts;
- six to eight blankets or large towels.

Lesson 3

Aims: to develop controlled walking balance; addressing sections 1–4 and 6d, 8a, 8b, 8c and 8d of Key Stage 1 National Curriculum PE programme of study.

Objectives

- to develop a sense of balance;
- to develop body awareness;
- to encourage controlled movement.

1   Review the work undertaken the previous week. Ask if the children had practised any of the activities at home, reiterate how it had been a very hard session yet they had succeeded very well. Introduce the aim of the session.

2   Warm up by moving slowly round the room in various directions as requested by the teacher, change pace and direction.

3   Give each child a beanbag, place this on the head and try to cross the room without it falling off.
4   Balance the beanbag on the head and try to walk along a line marked on the floor using coloured tape.
5   In small teams practise walking along a trail created by the teacher which consists of a coloured tape which is zigzagged across the room, a pathway drawn in chalk, a winding skipping rope. Children will be encouraged to place feet precisely one foot in front of the other along the trail.
6   In small teams give a number of items, namely: a skipping rope, coloured chalk, coloured insulation tape. Each group must make a trail for other groups to follow which incorporates straight lines, curves, loops, etc. They are then marked by the founding group on control and balance.
7   To conclude, play a game of 'frozen beanbag'. Each child places a beanbag on the head and moves around the room according to the teacher's instructions. If the beanbag topples, the child becomes frozen! They can only be defrosted if a fellow classmate comes and picks up his beanbag and replaces it on their head without their own beanbag falling off. The winner is the child who has helped the most people.
8   Conclude by discussing whether it made them more aware of how much control was needed to balance on a narrow line, and how this would help them to control movements in general to help coordinate around a variety of obstacles.

Equipment needed

- one beanbag per child;
- six to eight skipping ropes (without handles);
- eight rolls of colour insulation tape;
- a variety of coloured chalks.

Lesson 4

Aim: to further develop balance but incorporating spatial concepts above and below; addressing sections 1–4 and 6d, 8a, 8b, 8c and 8d of Key Stage 1 National Curriculum PE programme of study.

Objectives

- to develop coordination and spatial planning;
- to encourage group cohesion and cooperation;
- to encourage teamwork and creative planning.

1   Revisit the last session by asking a member of the class to demonstrate how they had to walk along a narrow trail carefully. Inform the class that this would be developed during this session and they would have to be able to balance and judge distances.
2   The teacher creates an obstacle course where children have to climb over a series of low obstacles to get to the other side. The children have to follow the teacher's lead in climbing over all the obstacles to reach the finishing post.

3 Divide the group into small teams, the team must hold hands and go around the obstacle course without breaking hands. This is repeated at speed and timed using a stopwatch by the teacher.
   NB: The child with dyspraxia is supported in this activity by being placed between two competent athletes; by holding hands the child can feel supported and less vulnerable to tripping.

4 The children are given a series of cards which states 'under' or 'over'. Each team has to make an obstacle course which incorporates the transfer beneath or over an object. The team then challenges another group to get through their course in a selected number of seconds (the teacher must monitor that the challenge in terms of timescale is realistic). The challenging team must complete the course with hands held.

5 Conclude with a game of pirates using only the mats.

6 Discuss how it felt to be physically joined as a group to undertake these exercises. What were the benefits? Discuss corporate learning.

Equipment needed

• a series of objects to step over, such as cones, gym bench;
• a series of objects to climb under, such as low tables, blankets held at either side with weights, nets or parachute silk;
• cards with the words and picture representing 'under' and 'over';
• mats or carpet squares.

Lesson 5

Aims: to develop the theme of balance *and* movement addressing sections 1–4 and 6a, 6b, 6c, 6d, 8a, 8b, 8c and 8d of Key Stage 1 National Curriculum PE programme of study.

Objectives

• introduce awareness of movement and rhythm;
• create sequences of movement which incorporate different movement planes, direction, speed and balance;
• encourage teamwork;
• encourage creative dance.

1 Discuss last week's session and inform class that today the activities are going to combine both shoulder and hip stability and balance, but this week's will incorporate music.

2 Warm up using slow music and movement routine.

3 Position children on their mats sitting on the floor, play a sample of music and ask the children to move their upper limbs in a variety of directions according to the music.

4 Each child selects a space on the floor. The teacher puts on some music and asks the children to say what the music reminds them of. The teacher then replays

the music and when the child is touched lightly on the shoulder they are allowed to move according to the music. Several children can be touched at one time, when touched again they must freeze; therefore the teacher is constantly touching and freezing children. This means that only four or five children will be moving at the same time. This helps to control space, enabling the child with spatial deficits to cope with manoeuvring around children. It also helps the remaining children to consider their movements carefully and create an imaginative routine.

5   Children are paired, a further piece of music is played and each pair must create a short movement routine based on that music. The rule is that they must maintain physical contact with each other, i.e. hold hands, or work on the floor touching feet, or create a routine back to back. These brief dance sequences are shared with the class.

6   Three sets of pairs are combined to create groups of approximately six children. Each group must invent a machine. For example; a bubble-making machine, a combine harvester, a sweet-making machine. Group members must create parts of the machine which must connect in some way each other. Movements can include squatting, balancing on one leg, clapping, rotations, etc. The machines are presented to the rest of the group.

7   The class concludes with a discussion regarding how each movement has connected together and how the dances and machines were reliant on cooperative working to make the activity successful.

Equipment required

* CD player;
* a range of music without vocals.

Lesson 6

Aims: to develop body awareness addressing sections 1–4 and 6a, 6b, 6c, 6d, 8a, 8b, 8c and 8d of Key Stage 1 National Curriculum PE programme of study.

Objectives

* to develop a personal awareness of limb position and controlled movement;
* to develop group cooperation;
* to develop creative thinking.

1   Explain how the last session involved each child moving their bodies in time to the music and how the session expected children to use their imagination and creative energy. Discuss how this lesson intends to expand this knowledge by helping the children to become aware of their body position and how to control movement.

2   Warm up. The teacher asks the children to jog slowly around the room. When stop is called, the teacher will call out 'tall', all children must try to look as tall as possible which will involve standing on tiptoes and stretching arms up in the air. When 'go' is called children resort to jogging again. Repeat using the

commands: 'small', 'wide', 'spiky', 'thin', and 'round'. At the end of the warm-up describe how this lesson involved movement and using the body to create shapes and objects.

3   Everyone chooses a partner; take it in turn to mirror your partner's actions. Use certain children as examples of good observation.

4   In small teams copy the actions of the person in front who will move around the room incorporating the diverse movement planes and directions required in the warm-up.

5   Each child stands on his mat. The teacher calls out a letter shape and each child moves their body to that shape.

6   Place children in groups of three; give a simple three-lettered word. Children should position their bodies to create the word. The rest of the class must guess what the word is.

7   The children must select their own word and position their bodies so that the class can 'read' the word. This is a creative, cooperative activity which requires considerable body awareness.

8   Discuss how this lesson helps the children to not only control their bodies but consider letter forms, words and team cooperation.

Equipment required

*   carpet mats.

Lesson 7

Aim: to develop ball skills addressing sections 1–4 and 7a, 7b, 7c, 7d, 8a, 8b and 8c of Key Stage 1 National Curriculum PE programme of study.

Objectives

*   to develop spatial awareness;
*   to develop size constancy in order to assess the size and speed of an object, i.e. balloon or ball;
*   to develop team cooperation.

1   Ask children to reiterate what they learned from the previous lesson where they used their bodies as letter shapes. Explain that this session will be particularly helpful in developing ball skills.

2   Arrange each child in pairs. Sit child opposite a partner on the floor with legs apart, and feet touching those of the partner. Provide each child with a football. Roll the ball from one to another using a different part of the upper body, i.e. the hand, fist, wrist, elbow and forearm.

3   Pairs stand up and hold hands. Try to roll the ball across from one person's arms to the next. Try to roll the ball backwards and forwards ten times without the ball falling.

4   Create two lines on the floor, 3 metres apart, with a partner standing behind each line facing their partner. Provide half the children with a balloon. Pass the

balloon to each other. Once this has been successfully passed three times, one of the pair takes a step backwards and repeats the exercise. Continue until it is impossible to pass the balloon any further.

5   Repeat the activity described above but use a soft sponge ball.

6   Form the class into small groups of three children. Create a squared-off area using either coloured insulation tape or chalk approximately 4 × 4 metres. Each team has a balloon of a similar colour, i.e. team one has three green balloons, and team two has three red balloons. Select two teams to start the game. Children stand in the square and must keep the balloons in the air at all times. If the balloon lands on the floor it is taken out. If the balloon is hit outside the square it is also out. The winners are the team that has their balloon remaining. Repeat this game with other teams.

7   Finish session with a game of balloon volleyball in teams of six players.

8   Cool down with a discussion regarding why the children thought balloons were used. Explain the difference in speed of a balloon compared to a ball, and the effort needed to get a balloon to move a distance. Suggest that games such as swingball will help to develop ball skills. Encourage practice at home.

Equipment needed

- chalk or coloured insulation tape;
- coloured balloons;
- a volley ball net or equivalent;
- footballs (enough for half the class).

Lesson 8

Aims: to develop upper limb control and shoulder girdle stability addressing sections 1–4 and 6a, 8a, 8b, 8c and 8d of Key Stage 1 National Curriculum PE programme of study.

Objectives

- to develop shoulder girdle stability;
- to increase proprioception in the upper limbs;
- to develop upper limb control.

1   Ask the children which part of the body was mostly involved in the previous session (upper limb control). Explain how this lesson will develop upper limb control further by building up the strength and stamina in the upper limbs.

2   Warm-up. Sit on the floor with legs straight. Complete a short exercise routine.

3   Lie in prone and attempt ladies press-ups.

4   Commando-crawl from one side of the room to another.

5   Create an obstacle course using cones, tubes and blankets, crawl through the course in the commando position.

6   Divide class into small teams, take it in turns to lie on scooterboard or skateboard and propel using hands only. Control the number of people moving simultaneously to avoid fingers being run over.

7   Create an obstacle course: encourage each team to complete the course while lying prone, using arms to propel themselves across the room.

8   Discuss how this session has strengthened their shoulder girdle and upper limb movements, which will help when attempting upper limb activities such as throwing and catching, and fine-motor activities such as handwriting.

Equipment required

- scooterboards can be made simply by attaching four rotating castors to the base of a smooth board, i.e. a large chopping board.
- alternatively ask some of the children to bring in either their own or a relative's skateboard for the lesson;
- cones for goalposts.

Lesson 9

Aims: to develop hand–eye coordination addressing sections 1–4 and 7a, 7b, 7c, 7d, 8a, 8b, 8c and 8d of Key Stage 1 National Curriculum PE programme of study.

Objectives

- to develop controlled hand–eye coordination;
- to develop spatial awareness;
- to develop accurate targeting of an object.

1   Discuss how strength in the shoulder girdle (the focus of the previous lesson) helps to develop control in the arms. Explain this lesson will develop upper limb control as well as the ability to move and judge distances.

2   Warm-up. Two lines are drawn across the room with a distance of 2 metres between. The class is divided in two with each half standing behind each line; each child facing a partner. Half the class is given beanbags and must shove these across the floor to his partner. This is returned in a similar way. The beanbag is shoved across three times by each child, after which one row of children take a step back making the distance between wider by approximately 0.5 metres. Continue until it becomes too difficult to project the beanbag.

3   Each child is given an indoor hockey stick. Four 'goal' areas are set up using cones. A cross is marked on the floor 3 metres away from the goal. The class are then divided into four teams and each team member must take it in turns to place their beanbag on the marked cross and shove the beanbag into the goal using the indoor hockey stick. The winning team is the group who have scored the most goals in the allotted time.

4   Repeat the activity described above but this time the team start at the opposite end of the room to the goal area. The children push the beanbag across the room using the indoor hockey stick; when they reach the goal area, they attempt to hit the beanbag into the goal. Once a goal is scored the player runs back to the next person and tags them to indicate the start of their turn. NB: the weight of the beanbag ensures that it is easier to control.

5 Do the same as above but manoeuvre beanbags around a series of obstacles such as cones.
6 Form four or five small teams of approximately five or six players. Play a game of floor hockey; this uses a beanbag which must remain on the floor and must be shoved across into the goal. Change teams when a goal has been scored.
7 Review progress of session and encourage children to practise this at home using a tennis ball and hockey stick made from a rolled newspaper.

Equipment required

•   enough indoor hockey sticks for whole class;
•   alternatively make stiff batons using sheets of newspaper and tape; fold the end to create an elbow to act as the hook;
•   a beanbag for each class member;
•   eight cones to act as goalposts;
•   insulating tape or chalk to serve as distance markers.

Lesson 10

Aim: to develop foot–eye coordination addressing sections 1–4 and 7a, 7b, 7c, 7d, 8a, 8b, 8c and 8d of Key Stage 1 National Curriculum PE programme of study.

Objectives

•   to develop ability to balance on either leg;
•   to develop foot–eye coordination;
•   to develop controlled movement.

1 Discuss the importance of balance in sporting activities and how we must be able to transfer our weight from one foot to another, especially when playing games such as football. Explain that this lesson will help to improve controlled balance.
2 Place a rope in a straight line across the gym; encourage children to start by walking along the rope with one foot in front of the other, following a leader.
3 Return along the rope but this time placing a foot either side of the rope.
4 Repeat this but increase speed.
5 Add an additional rope 0.75 metres apart and in parallel to the original rope. Children must run along with feet either side of the rope so they are swaying to and fro when they run.
6 Widen the gap to 0.5 metres, and repeat this activity. This will require each child to balance from one leg to another while moving forward to the other end of the room. (Rope can be widened again if the children are older/taller.)
7 Explain that the previous activities were making children hop from one leg to another while moving forward and this was necessary to play football.
8 Give each child a beanbag, and set up a series of cone goalposts around the room. Highlight a spot some 3 metres from the goal. In small groups the children must attempt to kick the beanbag into the goal from the allocated spot. Increase complexity by having a run up to the beanbag. Increase distance from the goal.

9   To conclude have a game of beanbag football in small teams.
10 Discuss with children how a beanbag helps them to learn controlled footwork and how with practice they can progress to using a ball. Encourage children to practise dribbling with a beanbag before trying to control a ball.

Equipment needed

- two long washing-line-type ropes;
- cones or markers to act as goalposts;
- a beanbag each.

As with any programme there is a need to be sensitive to the requirements of individual children and flexibility to adapt the programme according to the group's abilities and interpersonal dynamics. Therefore the order of this programme may be changed if necessary. On conclusion of this programme skills can be further developed by collaborative planning between occupational therapist or physiotherapist and teacher. Further ideas for relevant activities can be found in books such as Chia et al. (1996) and Bissell et al. (1998).

The programme described has been used effectively with a whole class of pupils which included two children with dyspraxia; all were able to benefit from the activities and enjoyed the more unusual pieces of equipment such as the blankets and scooterboards. However, each group of children differs and it is important to consider the different ways activities can be used to ensure that *all* children are included in class PE lessons. Black and Haskins (1996) suggest three ways to structure activities so that this is achieved:

1   Parallel activity – this is where children play the same game altogether but in their own way. For example if the aim is to develop hopping, and several children are able to hop well, than practice may be set for them to hop along a precise line or within hoops, whereas other children may struggle to balance on each leg so activities such as rocking from one leg to another across a marked line may be more appropriate for them. The children have the same goal but are using differing strategies to achieve this goal.
2   Inclusive adapted activity – where there is opportunity for all children to participate in adapted versions of games and activities. There are several examples of this within the programme provided. For example, in Lesson 9 a beanbag is used rather than a ball. This aims to develop control, which may not be achieved if all children used a ball and indoor hockey stick.
3   Discrete adapted activity – this is where children participate together in pairs or practise individually. For example if the game involves learning to maintain a ball in the air using a bat, a child with dyspraxia may be given a balloon rather than a tennis ball.

These three methods of adaptation can determine a child's success in physical education.

As children reach Key Stages 4 and 5 of the National Curriculum there is more emphasis on more refined movements, competitive sports and complex gymnastics

e setting

eanbag football in small teams.
eanbag helps them to learn controlled footwork
n progress to using a ball. Encourage children to
bag before trying to control a ball.

pes;
posts;

a need to be sensitive to the requirements of
o adapt the programme according to the group's
s. Therefore the order of this programme may be
n of this programme skills can be further devel-
tween occupational therapist or physiotherapist
ant activities can be found in books such as Chia

en used effectively with a whole class of pupils
dyspraxia; all were able to benefit from the
usual pieces of equipment such as the blankets
group of children differs and it is important
ities can be used to ensure that *all* children are
k and Haskins (1996) suggest three ways to
ieved:

children play the same game altogether but in
f the aim is to develop hopping, and several
an practice may be set for them to hop along a
ereas other children may struggle to balance on
cking from one leg to another across a marked
r them. The children have the same goal but are
ieve this goal.
here there is opportunity for all children to
s of games and activities. There are several
gramme provided. For example, in Lesson 9 a
ll. This aims to develop control, which may not
a ball and indoor hockey stick.
s where children participate together in pairs or
le if the game involves learning to maintain a
l with dyspraxia may be given a balloon rather

can determine a child's success in physical

d 5 of the National Curriculum there is more
ts, competitive sports and complex gymnastics

balloon to each other. Once this has been successfully passed three times, one of the pair takes a step backwards and repeats the exercise. Continue until it is impossible to pass the balloon any further.

5   Repeat the activity described above but use a soft sponge ball.
6   Form the class into small groups of three children. Create a squared-off area using either coloured insulation tape or chalk approximately 4 × 4 metres. Each team has a balloon of a similar colour, i.e. team one has three green balloons, and team two has three red balloons. Select two teams to start the game. Children stand in the square and must keep the balloons in the air at all times. If the balloon lands on the floor it is taken out. If the balloon is hit outside the square it is also out. The winners are the team that has their balloon remaining. Repeat this game with other teams.
7   Finish session with a game of balloon volleyball in teams of six players.
8   Cool down with a discussion regarding why the children thought balloons were used. Explain the difference in speed of a balloon compared to a ball, and the effort needed to get a balloon to move a distance. Suggest that games such as swingball will help to develop ball skills. Encourage practice at home.

Equipment needed

- chalk or coloured insulation tape;
- coloured balloons;
- a volley ball net or equivalent;
- footballs (enough for half the class).

Lesson 8

Aims: to develop upper limb control and shoulder girdle stability addressing sections 1–4 and 6a, 8a, 8b, 8c and 8d of Key Stage 1 National Curriculum PE programme of study.

Objectives

- to develop shoulder girdle stability;
- to increase proprioception in the upper limbs;
- to develop upper limb control.

1   Ask the children which part of the body was mostly involved in the previous session (upper limb control). Explain how this lesson will develop upper limb control further by building up the strength and stamina in the upper limbs.
2   Warm-up. Sit on the floor with legs straight. Complete a short exercise routine.
3   Lie in prone and attempt ladies press-ups.
4   Commando-crawl from one side of the room to another.
5   Create an obstacle course using cones, tubes and blankets, crawl through the course in the commando position.
6   Divide class into small teams, take it in turns to lie on scooterboard or skateboard and propel using hands only. Control the number of people moving simultaneously to avoid fingers being run over.

7   Create an obstacle course: encourage each team to complete the course while lying prone, using arms to propel themselves across the room.
8   Discuss how this session has strengthened their shoulder girdle and upper limb movements, which will help when attempting upper limb activities such as throwing and catching, and fine-motor activities such as handwriting.

Equipment required

* scooterboards can be made simply by attaching four rotating castors to the base of a smooth board, i.e. a large chopping board.
* alternatively ask some of the children to bring in either their own or a relative's skateboard for the lesson;
* cones for goalposts.

Lesson 9

Aims: to develop hand–eye coordination addressing sections 1–4 and 7a, 7b, 7c, 7d, 8a, 8b, 8c and 8d of Key Stage 1 National Curriculum PE programme of study.

Objectives

* to develop controlled hand–eye coordination;
* to develop spatial awareness;
* to develop accurate targeting of an object.

1   Discuss how strength in the shoulder girdle (the focus of the previous lesson) helps to develop control in the arms. Explain this lesson will develop upper limb control as well as the ability to move and judge distances.
2   Warm-up. Two lines are drawn across the room with a distance of 2 metres between. The class is divided in two with each half standing behind each line; each child facing a partner. Half the class is given beanbags and must shove these across the floor to his partner. This is returned in a similar way. The beanbag is shoved across three times by each child, after which one row of children take a step back making the distance between wider by approximately 0.5 metres. Continue until it becomes too difficult to project the beanbag.
3   Each child is given an indoor hockey stick. Four 'goal' areas are set up using cones. A cross is marked on the floor 3 metres away from the goal. The class are then divided into four teams and each team member must take it in turns to place their beanbag on the marked cross and shove the beanbag into the goal using the indoor hockey stick. The winning team is the group who have scored the most goals in the allotted time.
4   Repeat the activity described above but this time the team start at the opposite end of the room to the goal area. The children push the beanbag across the room using the indoor hockey stick; when they reach the goal area, they attempt to hit the beanbag into the goal. Once a goal is scored the player runs back to the next person and tags them to indicate the start of their turn. NB: the weight of the beanbag ensures that it is easier to control.

9   To conclude have a game of b
10   Discuss with children how a l
     and how with practice they ca
     practise dribbling with a bean

Equipment needed

* two long washing-line-type ro
* cones or markers to act as goal
* a beanbag each.

As with any programme there is
individual children and flexibility t
abilities and interpersonal dynamic
changed if necessary. On conclusi
oped by collaborative planning be
and teacher. Further ideas for relev
et al. (1996) and Bissell et al. (1998).
     The programme described has b
which included two children wit
activities and enjoyed the more un
and scooterboards. However, eac
to consider the different ways activ
included in class PE lessons. Bla
structure activities so that this is ac

1   Parallel activity – this is where
     their own way. For example
     children are able to hop well, t
     precise line or within hoops, wh
     each leg so activities such as r
     line may be more appropriate f
     using differing strategies to ach
2   Inclusive adapted activity – v
     participate in adapted versior
     examples of this within the pr
     beanbag is used rather than a ba
     be achieved if all children used
3   Discrete adapted activity – this
     practise individually. For exam
     ball in the air using a bat, a chil
     than a tennis ball.

These three methods of adaptatior
education.
     As children reach Key Stages 4 a
emphasis on more refined movemer

involving the use of apparatus; in addition swimming, athletics and outdoor adventurous activities are recommended. It is often the increase in competitive activity that can completely throw the confidence of children with dyspraxia. It is at this point that many excuses will be heard to avoid PE which may include the child actually 'using' their condition to avoid certain activities. It is at this time more than any other that sporting activities can be adapted not to highlight the needs of the pupils with specific difficulties but to demonstrate the variety of ways certain sports can be played, increasing pupils' awareness of what it is like to experience movement and coordination difficulties.

Consider the following example of how a simple game of volleyball can be altered to provide opportunity, and extend specific movement skills.

Rules of play	Adaptation of activity	Equipment for adaptation	Purpose of adaptation
6 players in each team	Reduce the number of players in the team to 4 or less	None	To assist spatial organisation
A heavy volleyball is used	Alter density of ball, i.e. use a sponge ball, light-weight ball or balloon	Balloons Soft sponge ball Light football	Slows down the motion and speed of the 'ball'; allowing those who need time to assess distances to do so. Texture of alternatives makes them easier to catch
Net is hung at a height of between 2.2 and 2.4 metres	Lower the height of the net	Adaptable volleyball posts	Enables pupils to judge distances at eye height rather than above eye-level, which can be more difficult
The court is 18 × 9 metres with each half being 9 × 9 metres	Reduce the size of the court	Adapt with coloured insulation tape or chalk	Assists spatial planning and organisation
	Seat all players on chairs		Prevents personal invasion of space

continued

Rules of play	Adaptation of activity	Equipment for adaptation	Purpose of adaptation
			Limits movement while extending range of upper limb movement.
Three passes are allowed before the ball must be passed over the net	Allow the ball to be passed to more than three players	None	Accommodates slow motor processing
The ball is not allowed to touch the floor	Allow the ball to bounce once	None	Enables child to judge the speed and distance of object more easily
The ball is not allowed to be held on any part of the body	Allow ball to be held before being passed or projected forward	None	Accommodates slow motor planning and processing
15 points and a 2 point advantage are required to win the game	State that winning team need only get 10 points plus 2 point advantage	None	Less effort required as the game will be shorter

Many other sporting activities can be adapted in a similar way and the novelty can be very stimulating for children, particularly for those who become quite bored of traditional sports.

In addition to the specific adaptations and the recommended programme, there are a range of general strategies which can be easily implemented into the class PE curriculum which will help the child with dyspraxia to appreciate and enjoy PE, these are outlined in the following sections.

General pointers to help with physical education

- Give the child adequate time to get ready for PE.

Joel struggled to manage the small fastenings of his school shirt; this slowed him down considerably when getting changed for PE. This frustrated him immensely and his teachers asked if I could offer any advice. I showed his mum how to change him into Superman!

We took the buttons off his school shirt and sewed them on top of his button holes. Underneath we sewed small rounds of Velcro, with the matching Velcro rounds being positioned on the removed button site. When the Velcro pieces were connected it appeared that he was wearing a 'normal' shirt with buttons fastened appropriately.

At the cuffs, we removed the buttons and reattached these by creating an elastic stalk. Therefore Joel was able to remove his arms from his sleeves without undoing the cuffs.

His trouser-fly zip was rather small and fiddly, but rather than wear jogging trousers, which was not in keeping with school uniform, we attached a short, matching coloured shoelace to his trouser zip, so that instead of struggling to pinch the small zip head, he could grasp the string and pull down. The top button was replaced with a Velcro circle, which reduced the need to manage a fiddly button.

During the winter months, on the days he took PE, he wore his school gym t-shirt instead of his vest.

With these adaptations in place, Joel became the first to get ready for PE. These small adaptations made such a difference to Joel's confidence and eliminated the humiliation he previously experienced in getting dressed with his peers.

- Identify a clear lesson goal for the lesson and, with the children, review at the end of the session whether this has been achieved. That is, goal: to develop an understanding of left and right (orientation). To develop ability to catch an object 3 metres away.
- Restrict the working area by marking out spaces using chalk or positioning gym benches. Sometimes the sheer size of a gymnasium can be daunting to many children, and often the whole hall is not required. Restricting the space can help *all* children control movements.
- Limit items in the room if possible, to reduce distractibility.
- Reduce echoing noises such as air-conditioning fans if this means that you, as a teacher, are shouting to be heard above the noise.
- Check the room temperature: cold children tend not to move!
- Give each child his own space by either marking the floor, providing a hoop or carpet square, which will be their allocated space.
- 'Ground' the children by encouraging them to return to their own mat after each activity, this helps to control space and is less intimidating to the child with dyspraxia.
- Learn movements in small stages, building up gradually to sequential patterns of movement.
- Start each session by reminding pupils of the previous lesson's learning outcomes. The child with dyspraxia may attend each PE lesson in trepidation: by reiterating previous achievements, some of the fears can be alleviated.

- After reminding pupils of previous achievements, structure each session with an introduction, warm-up, main activity/ies, and conclude with a positive fun activity. Review whether goals have been achieved before getting changed back into uniform.
- Incorporate music as much as possible. All movement requires a sense of rhythm and the awareness of this will not only help the child with dyspraxia but will benefit all children.
- Some children with dyspraxia will also have hypotonia (low muscle tone) and may have 'flat feet'. Activities which require lower limb propulsion such as running, jumping and hopping will be particularly difficult for these children, especially in bare feet. Allow wearing of trainers with insoles if these have been provided, be aware that children may resort to going on their tiptoes to increase propulsion. Be aware that children with flat feet will tire more quickly than other children.
- Grade all activities very carefully.
- Be aware that children with dyspraxia will use a variety of tactics to 'get out' of doing a task they feel they may fail in. This may be more evident in team games when they are aware that they could let their team down.
- Gradually increase strength and stamina, this will not be the same in children with dyspraxia compared to their peers, therefore later activities may warrant some discrete adaptation.
- Use pictures at certain activity stations to illustrate and reinforce the task.
- Use lines or spots on the floor to identify paths.
- Use positive reinforcement at every opportunity.

It is hoped that the examples and recommendations given in this chapter will help you to understand physical education from the perspective of both teacher and therapist. It is in this key area of the curriculum that collaboration between professionals can be successful. However, if true inclusion of children with dyspraxia is to prevail it will require 'a *commitment* to teach, learn and work together across discipline boundaries to implement unified service plans' (Lomas and Lacey, 1993, p. 20). This will mean therapists spending time in the classroom, particularly during PE lessons appreciating the requirements of the National Curriculum, while teachers become open to flexible ways of thinking about how to engage children with motor coordination difficulties in the PE lesson in order to maximise, not only their potential, but the potential of all the pupils in the class.

Chapter 10

Dyspraxia and social skills

Children and young people with dyspraxia have a series of unique characteristics, which are explainable in terms of neurological maturity, dysfunctional perceptual acquisition and impaired motor development. With knowledge these are understandable. Unfortunately, children with dyspraxia often do not have the privilege of understanding and accepting peers, who embrace diversity and difference. Behaviour which is out of the ordinary is often treated with ridicule and contempt at a time when individuals themselves are struggling to form their own identity.

Parents who do not have dyspraxia themselves are able to observe, compare and describe characteristics, which differ from the norm; they can also see what needs to be done to conform. However, the child with dyspraxia is not in that fortunate position and only knows that he operates differently from his peers because he is constantly told so. This awareness increases as more and more errors and incompetences are highlighted. The fact that the child struggles to know how to change his patterns of behaviour reflects in his self-concept. In reality the difficulties of the child with dyspraxia exist only because they are compared to what society describes as 'normal'. To explain this more clearly, a child who is born without an arm does *not* have a problem. He has only known what it is like to have one arm and quickly learns to accommodate and adapt to living within a two-handed society. The only 'problem' this child experiences is that imposed by society. This is reflected in comments frequently made such as 'poor thing', 'what a shame' and 'what a pity' which are derogatory and debasing. These terms, which are often said in innocence, imply that children born with differences should be pitied and are a shame. Pity is unwelcome and unnecessary. In contrast a child who is born with two limbs, who suffers an accident and loses an arm, can appropriately claim to have a problem. This child knew what it was like to have two arms, had skills which required two limbs and had a self-perception based around this image. The loss of a limb limits independence and so solutions to this barrier are sought.

Similarly children with dyspraxia see themselves in a certain way, and respond according to their self-perception. However, as this does not fit into the norm, their perceived incompetence is pointed out frequently with a request that the child might do something to rectify the situation. There is less chance of acquiring the sympathy given to those with a visible physical impediment. Instead the child is repeatedly told to change with the absence of suggestions as to why they should and how! How can a child feel valued if he is constantly being asked to change?

The consequence of this frequent call to amend is a child who is not only struggling to conform to the pressure of education, home life, and social situations, but who is also battling with the challenges issued by his peers that they must 'fit' or be rejected. The strain will often cause extreme anxiety, which effects both social interaction and self-confidence. The psychological effects of dyspraxia have far-reaching implications for learning in that a child who has few friends, who has a low-self image and little self-esteem will have little confidence when attempting classwork.

The effect of low self-esteem and confidence is a child who lacks self-worth, who withdraws from potentially conflicting situations with others, who becomes socially isolated and fearful of new situations. In extreme cases some children refuse to attend school, become depressed and are at risk from self-harm. At the opposite end of the spectrum, other children cope with constant criticism by confrontation and aggression. Some children play truant and are vulnerable to delinquency.

In general, however, children with dyspraxia do persist at school but struggle throughout their educational experiences with peer relationships. In the early years young boys with dyspraxia are often 'adopted' by the girls in the class who manipulate them into playing their games. Friendships may be limited, and the child may affiliate themselves with a child with comparable difficulties or who is similarly vulnerable, and consequently the risk from bullying is high. Gender differences are highlighted when they are rejected from games of football. Unfortunately children can be cruel and tactless and rejection from physical games is expressed as 'you can't play 'cos your rubbish!', rather than an appreciation of poor motor coordination.

The consequence of social separation or withdrawal is that the child often has poor social interaction and is unaware or unused to adopting certain social protocol. No matter what our personal views are on 'normalisation' and individuality, in today's society social etiquette is still an essential prerequisite in instigating and maintaining social relationships. Therefore appropriate social skills are essential to any child wishing to be 'included' in their home, local community, school and future workplace.

Social skills are characterised by 'abilities' and 'behaviour' and include: 'The ability to interact with others in a given social context in specific ways that are socially acceptable or valued and at the same time personally beneficial, mutually beneficial, or beneficial primarily to others' (Combs and Slaby, 1977, p. 162). This suggests that there is a vast array of expected behaviours, which differ according to circumstances and contexts. For example it is acceptable to eat with a knife and fork in most restaurants and cafes but would be inappropriate when eating in McDonald's. Much social behaviour is obscure and lacks rationale; for example, in England, as a young person, it is appropriate to shake hands with an adult when first introduced. But it would be inappropriate to greet a similar aged child in this way.

There are three contexts where social behaviours are learned within the family, within society and among peers. Family values incorporate expected behaviours which are demonstrated and taught within a family situation but which may differ from family to family. These social skills are based on parental expectations, and may vary in importance according to each responsible adult in the family unit. For example, the use of 'please' and 'thank you'; the need to eat together as a family; acceptance of discipline are taught values which determine a child's behaviour.

Acceptance or rejection of these 'rules' can affect family relationships. A couple who have quite high expectations of acceptable family behaviour may struggle with the behaviours of a child with dyspraxia and become frustrated and even embarrassed by their child's habits. Poor oral control may make meal times uncomfortable to other family members; clumsiness may influence the child's acceptance and involvement in playing games. Poor oral and personal hygiene may influence sibling relationships and the constant need for reassurance or clarification may be extremely frustrating to the child's carers.

Societal standards are also important; however the origins and purpose of many of these are also obscure. These are taught by example and demonstration and are very much context based. They have a cultural bias and may alter according to geographic location. It is no wonder that many children with dyspraxia struggle to even recognise social behaviours let alone conform to these. For example it is expected that if there are a number of people waiting to be served in a shop that a queue is formed, and individuals wait patiently for their respective turn. If you struggle to stand still or feel uncomfortable being in such close proximity to people as many young people with dyspraxia do, acceptable behaviour will immediately be challenged. Likewise it is accepted that conversation is kept to a minimum in a public library and any conversation is spoken at low volume. A child with dyspraxia may struggle to control the volume of his speech and so immediately draws attention to himself initiating disapproval by other library users.

Difficulties meeting peer expectations are the biggest source of concern for the majority of children with dyspraxia. Peer acceptance is extremely important to developing self-worth and social acceptance, yet young people's expectations are extremely high and non-conformation to these reaps the harshest sentence of social isolation and rejection.

As we learn much social behaviour through observing others, a child with dyspraxia may have the cognitive understanding of what would be desirable social behaviours but may not be able to translate the behaviour into action. For children with dyspraxia, dysfunctional perception particularly and poor coordination can seriously impede the acquisition of many social skills, which can have a significant effect on the development of interpersonal relationships. In particular children with dyspraxia will have the difficulties with communication and social skills that are covered in the following sections.

Difficulties with communication and social skills

Difficulties initiating conversations and discussions

Children with dyspraxia have no physical reason (unless they have verbal dyspraxia) why they should struggle to initiate conversation. However, constant correction of actions and public behaviour can take its toll on a child's confidence and this in turn can affect a child's ability to make friends and develop close relationships. Therefore difficulties in initiating conversations are often due to a lack of confidence rather than the inability to converse. In children where self-belief is lacking, eye contact may be poor and body language may portray their anxiety and social isolation. They therefore need encouragement to develop their confidence to initiate conversations and may also need guidance as to rules of communication, i.e. when to speak, when to listen, etc.

Children with verbal dyspraxia will have more pronounced communication problems and may not be able to initiate conversation spontaneously, despite being able to respond automatically to occasional questions. Children with verbal dyspraxia will portray more communication difficulties when put under pressure, or put on the spot than on other occasions.

Limited repertoire of conversation topics

As many children with dyspraxia struggle with so many physical activities they frequently resign themselves to developing expertise or particular interests in one or two areas. The only hitch is that many children almost seem obsessed with certain activities or events to the negation of all others; to their peers this can become quite tedious, to adults quite irritating.

> Lucy at the age of 8 years was quite overweight. Her poor physical co-ordination meant that she struggled with many sporting activities and tired quickly. A lack of refined fine-motor skills also limited Lucy's leisure pursuits as board games, computer games and craft activities required more dexterity than Lucy could afford. Consequently much of Lucy's free time involved watching TV, especially football, and eating! Her parents, conscious of her vulnerability to gain weight encouraged her to swim as much as possible, but poor stamina and a low metabolic rate counteracted the benefits of this form of exercise. Lucy's solace was in food and her main topic of conversation usually was based around what she was having for tea, what other people would be having for their meals, favourite food, etc. Initially the simple question asked 'what are you having for tea?' seemed reasonable but then came an analysis of puddings, drinks, favourite brands, meals for the next few days, packed lunch contents, etc. Understandably it was very easy to get thoroughly exasperated with the conversation.

Poor 'volume control'

Children with dyspraxia lack the fine-tuning in the way they interpret sensory information and may also have difficulties with auditory discrimination (listening only to that which is relevant/important). This can result in the child being unaware when the TV volume control is too loud, or when they are speaking at a level above the crowd. Whispering can be particularly difficult to monitor, which can cause social embarrassment in situations where quietness is appropriate such as the library or within church. To help with volume adjustment, children with dyspraxia will often try to mimic those around them or generalise situations where the voice has been projected. This may indeed be inappropriate.

Jack noted that when his mum wanted to control his pet dog she would produce a terse retort of 'down' or 'sit'. Jack wishing to produce the same response to a toddler running around a McDonald's restaurant resorted to the same retort much to the amusement of all around and was completely disregarded by the child!

Difficulty expressing emotions

Having dyspraxia can be very confusing and wearisome especially when regular criticism is given for many simple actions. Constant prompts to change tactics without demonstration of how to can leave a child frustrated and fractious. The expression of this may be suppressed to breaking point when an emotional outburst may provide a release but may occur at a seemingly small irritation. Pent-up frustration may also lead to destructive outbursts or extreme responses.

Although emotions or feelings are private events, difficult to measure except through their overt behavioural expressions, the emotions and their manifestation have a role in social skills training. Undesirable behavioural manifestations of affect, i.e. rage, indicate a need for social skills training to teach alternate behaviours. Similarly fear, anxiety, shyness can interfere with learning and performing social behaviours. According to Feshbach *et al.* (1983) social skills training can enhance interpersonal relationships by focusing on:

* recognition and discrimination of feeling – the ability to use relevant information to label and identify emotions;
* perspective and role taking– the ability to understand that other individuals may see and interpret situations differently; the ability to assume and experience another's viewpoint and be aware of one's own emotions.

Poor body language and non-verbal responses

We have described how many children with dyspraxia have a poor self-image and often dysfunctional awareness of how they appear. This is not confined to their own self-perception but also their perception of others. This can be seen when you ask a child to draw another member of their family or friend. The drawing will often reflect their perception of the other person's appearance. Misguided observation of others can also lead to the child being unable to read the body language of those around them. As body language and non-verbal gestures are fundamental to many personal interactions this can have serious affects on relationships. Poor eye contact and a lack of detailed observation exacerbate this. For example many people's personal space can be invaded by those with poor spatial planning, subtleties of facial expressions can be misunderstood and gestures can be ignored. These difficulties however do not shelter the child from feeling rejection, mockery or ridicule. These add to the child's poor self-image and self-confidence exacerbating problems of eye contact and self-esteem.

Difficulties giving and receiving compliments

We learn to give and receive compliments by example and personal experience. People who seem to criticise constantly are often those who have previously been criticised themselves. This is also true of children with dyspraxia. If you are frequently informed of your mistakes and misdemeanours, you will struggle to believe or accept positive feedback. In addition, many children with dyspraxia who are placed in a situation such as a team activity where they know that they will either fail or hinder the team, may resort to sabotage by being unduly critical of the activity. This 'front' needs sensitive handling to determine the rationale behind certain behaviours.

Lack of assertiveness

Poor self-esteem and lack of self-confidence automatically impacts on the child's ability to express opinions or provide a rational argument for a situation, consequently many children with dyspraxia are either compliant, which will occasionally leave them appearing 'weak', or the opposite, defiant and obstreperous. This being an effective, albeit unpopular, strategy to avoid certain activities. Lack of assertion can leave the child feeling afraid in new situations and limited in their repertoire of activities undertaken. Help is needed to improve these skills in particular in order to help each child maximise his potential and to explore all the opportunities available to him. Children need considerable support and it may take several years of regular encouragement before the child can even contemplate and express a personal interest or desire. The following scenario occurred after one year of regular support and guidance.

> John was a shy little boy of 7 who had very low self-esteem and was extremely conscious that he was unable to do many of the things his peers could. His way to avoid any activity which looked potentially difficult was to feign illness. These he found were hard to dispute! He was probably the only member of his class who did not partake in some after-school club or activity. As his occupational therapist, it took over a year of input and support to build up his confidence and self-assertion to a point where he felt he could possibly try to develop a hobby or join a club.
>
> One day, John met me at his school and quietly sat next to me. He then cautiously asked if he could possibly learn how to play the piano. Being aware of his poor manual dexterity this was a formidable request but after reassuring him that he could have a go, together with his parents we scoured the area for an empathetic piano teacher who would teach him at a pace which he could follow. He soon realised his difficulties in acquiring this skill and decided to try judo. Again after a few sessions he returned to me saying that it wasn't for him. Eventually we found a small theatre company, which taught children mime, drama and singing. Numbers were small and John was encouraged to put the talents he had developed to avoid many difficult tasks to a positive

goal. He found his niche and went on to perform in small amateur productions much to the joy of his parents.

The reward for me as his occupational therapist was helping John to get to a position where he was willing to attempt many new tasks which he and we knew would be difficult. He attempted these and the experience and his strength was such that he learned to select those activities he could potentially be good at without giving up completely.

Poor self-monitoring or regulation (poor self-awareness)

As many children with dyspraxia are unable to read body language and non-verbal signs, they are also not very good at recognising when they should complete an interaction, when they should move on or when to cease talking. This poor self-monitoring can be very unpopular with peers whose responses can be blunt, to say the least.

Individual regulation involves self-monitoring, which is the ability to be able to assess a situation and to know when to commence, initiate or conclude a discussion. This requires good observation skills and the ability to report one's own behaviour, self-evaluation which involves the comparison between self-observed behaviour and societal performance standards, and self-instruction which is used to support problem-solving strategies mentally. For example a child may think 'What is it I have to do?' (*plan*) 'I need to turn to page 23 of my math book' (*action*) 'glad I heard that right' (*self-reinforcement*) 'I got it right, I did OK' (*self-evaluation*).

Often the fear of getting it wrong can impede a child's ability to self-regulate and self-evaluate and the child feels intrinsically negative. It is therefore easier to withdraw from social situations rather than face possible ridicule, which is why it is important to give the child considerable extrinsic praise to encourage regulation and support confidence.

Perspective-taking

It is hard to appreciate the perspective of others when you are struggling to develop a personal perspective; this is especially true when certain coping mechanisms or avoidance strategies are adopted to avoid certain tasks. Consequently many children may appear defensive rather than open to a rational argument. Any personal threat quickly has them resorting to the application of a protective stance. Consequently these mechanisms may need to be highlighted to the child and they may need to be literally taught how to accommodate alternative perspectives in order to maintain effective relationships at school, home or at work.

Poor problem-solving ability

In order to come up with a solution to a problem, a methodical strategy is required and plan formulated. As many children with dyspraxia struggle to plan and organise their actions, problem-solving abilities can seem erratic. This is regularly seen when a teacher gives a new piece of work. The child will often appear to mess about with his pencilcase, spend a considerable time getting out the most appropriate equipment and appear to fiddle with preparatory materials. This will appear muddled and chaotic. This is how the child is attempting to order the 'problem', in the form of a new task. The chaotic organisation does not only demonstrate poor organisation but is often used as a delaying tactic to give the child more time to assimilate and process the relevant information.

Poor attention or concentration

We have previously described in detail how many children with dyspraxia struggle to cope with the volume of visual and auditory information in their environment. These difficulties can lead to the child being unable to focus or attend to relevant information tending instead to focus on the many remaining attractions in the environment. Consequently it may appear that the child is not listening or is disinterested in the conversation, which can seriously impact on peer relationships. With adult–child relationships this can appear rude or impudent. They therefore need to be taught the art of effective communication and strategies to help to attend to interpersonal interactions.

Tendency to withdraw or opt out of things that may be too difficult

Children with dyspraxia know that they do not function in the same way as their peers, and they quickly learn how to withdraw or opt out of activities, which may demonstrate their inabilities. It is important to ascertain how to motivate each child in order to address these avoidance tactics.

Adam was a classic example.

Adam at the age of 6 was very conscious that his attempts at writing did not look remotely like his peers, and was illegible. The more he tried to form letters correctly, the worse it seemed to look. Adam was introduced to the *Write from the Start: A Perceptual–Motor Approach to Handwriting* programme (Teodorescu and Addy, 1996) and was really motivated to follow the programme in its entirety. The teacher's main concern was that whenever Adam was asked to undertake any writing task he immediately seemed to 'freeze', panic and then seek ways of opting out. His most effective method of avoidance was to shriek at the top of his voice thus disrupting the whole class, he did not cease until physically removed from the class, where he would have five minutes time-out until the teacher could get a chance to speak to him and calm him down. This was exceptionally frustrating to his teacher and a source of irritation to his peers. Adam was given considerable support and time to air his fears to his occupational therapist who suggested to his teacher that she would personally speak to Adam about any new activity which involved handwriting after she had given the whole class instruction, this would be supported by a class diary where the directions for the task would be written down. In addition alternative solutions to his handwriting difficulties were given. For example Adam was allowed to write only the key verbs required from the paragraph written, therefore a task such as describe the sky, would not be written in complete sentences but key descriptive words could be listed, such as blue, atmosphere, airspace, soft clouds, marshmallows. This would not preclude Adam from ever writing in sentences, rather, these could be developed either at home or when more time was available. In addition to adapting instructions, Adam had a reward chart so that every day that he did not shriek and disrupt the class, he would receive a star; a suitable reward was then arranged between school and home.

Another method of avoiding tasks which may appear difficult is sabotage. This can often be seen in team games and is a very effective method of avoidance. For example in a PE lesson a teacher states that there is going to be an obstacle course race and that the class will be divided into four teams, the winners are the team which completes the course the first. The child with dyspraxia perceives that the task will be too difficult and that they will inevitably let their team down. To avoid losing face and causing embarrassment, the child then jeers to the teacher; 'this is boring, this is a game for babies, isn't it a rubbish idea, can't we do proper PE'. The end result is that teacher becomes irritated and disciplines the child by telling him to sit at one side while the game is being played. Bingo! The child has successfully avoided the task!

Difficulties with teamwork

The consciousness of their difference can leave many children who have dyspraxia with a complex about their abilities. This makes team games more difficult as the child is very conscious, especially in competitive circles that they could easily let their team down by not being fast, quick or bright enough. Therefore encouragement is needed to convince each child that they have as much potential as the next person.

How then can we help children to get over these social handicaps and how can we help children develop and maintain effective communication and friendships? Based on the assumption that social skills are learned behaviours we can assume that poor social skills can be altered and appropriate skills taught.

Contingency management, modelling, coaching and cognitive problem-solving are methods, which can be used subtly by a sensitive teacher who is aware of the needs of a child with dyspraxia. They can use the classroom as a place to observe and promote positive interactions between children, to demonstrate, coach and promote positive social skills in the context of the school environment. Parents can also help a child develop these skills, being in a particularly good position to observe subtle changes in their child's behaviour, which can indicate struggles and achievements. Alternately a responsible and empathic adult can run groups designed to develop key social skills. These are useful, as social skills fundamentally require peer inter-action, which can be provided in a group setting. Social skills groups usually bring together young people with similar needs to teach specific skills using role-play, drama, games and challenges. However, one of the key concerns of those who teach social skills is that of skill generalisation. It may be possible to teach a certain skill in one context but the child is unable to translate it into others. It is therefore important that skills are reinforced across time, settings, tasks and subjects.

To develop an appropriate social skills course, it is important that the leader can create a relaxed atmosphere, is sensitive to group dynamics and uses a variety of teaching strategies. There are numerous programmes and books available to guide those who wish to develop such a group (see the Appendix), however these must be selected and used with great care, and the individual must fully appreciate the dynamics of group interaction.

The following is an example of one programme introduced recently to a group of young people with dyspraxia whose self-confidence and self-esteem was at rock bottom. The group was run by a paediatric occupational therapist and was located in a classroom rather than in a hospital setting.

The young people who attended were referred by their teachers or at the request of their parents, with their agreement. The group consisted of six boys and two girls. The young people were aged between 11 and 15. The group met once each week, after school for one hour for a period of eight weeks.

Session 1: Introductory

The initial session was spent introducing each young person to the purpose of the group, ice-breaking and introductory activities. When the leader felt that the young people started to feel comfortable with the group ethos and members, a self-esteem checklist was completed. This checklist by Maines and Robinson (1988) known as the B/G-Steem is very easy to use and non-threatening to children.

The session was interesting as very quickly each young person realised they were not alone in struggling with the demands of secondary education and, feeling rather inadequate and useless, the conversation seemed almost cathartic for many members. Some of the personal stories shared gave such an insight into the daily struggles of these children. The completion of the self-esteem inventory was more revealing, for example consider how Mark, aged 13 responded.

Mark scored fifteen on the self-esteem inventory, which places him in the very low self-esteem category.

Scoring using the B/G-Steem is very simple and provides an indication of the child's level of self-esteem along with his locus of control. Locus of control is the extent to which the child believes he is responsible for his own behaviour. In Mark's case his score placed him in the 'very low' category for self-esteem, and in the 'normal' category for locus of control. He wished to quantify some of his responses and informed the leader that schoolwork was poor because his hand-writing was so bad; he also intimated that most of his friends were much younger than himself and several did not go to the same school as him. Results were similar for other group members.

Figure 10.1 (opposite) Completed self-esteem inventory. (Form reproduced by kind permission, Lucky Duck Publishing Ltd)

Please answer all the questions by circling YES or NO

Name **Mark**   Age **13**   School –   Date –

1	Is your school work good?	YES	(NO)
2	Do you like being a boy?	(YES)	NO
3	Are you strong and healthy?	(YES)	NO
4	Does someone else always choose what you wear?	YES	(NO)
5	Do people get angry with you?	(YES)	NO
6	Do your parents think you behave well?	YES	(NO)
7	Do children like playing with you?	YES	(NO)
8	Are you very nice looking?	YES	(NO)
9	Are you as clever as other children?	YES	(NO)
10	Do you worry a lot?	(YES)	NO
11	Does the teacher notice when you work hard?	YES	(NO)
12	Do your parents make you feel silly?	YES	(NO)
13	Are you a fast runner?	YES	(NO)
14	Do children choose you to play with them?	YES	(NO)
15	Can you make your work better if you really try?	YES	NO?
16	Are you a good reader?	(YES)	NO
17	Are you good at looking after yourself?	(YES)	NO
18	Does your Mum or Dad like you to help them?	YES	(NO)
19	Do you choose your friends?	(YES)	NO
20	Do you worry about how you look?	(YES)	NO
21	Do you have a best friend?	(YES)	NO
22	Is your teacher pleased with your work?	YES	(NO)
23	Do you need a lot of help?	(YES)	NO
24	Are your parents usually fair?	(YES)	NO
25	If someone doesn't understand can you explain what you want?	(YES)	NO
26	Do you find sums hard?	YES	(NO)
27	Do you have nice clothes?	(YES)	NO
28	Are other children unkind to you?	(YES)	NO
29	Do other people decide everything about your life?	YES	(NO)
30	Are you the best looking in your class?	YES	(NO)
31	Are your parents proud of you?	YES	NO ?
32	Do you make lots of mistakes?	(YES)	NO
33	Do you think that wishing can make nice things happen?	YES	(NO)
34	Are your parents cross with you for no reason?	YES	(NO)
35	Would you like to be someone else?	YES	(NO)

Session 2: Non-verbal communication

The second session of the programme reiterated the purpose of the group, stressing that by the end of the programme each young person would be able to highlight his individual personal qualities; emphasising the characteristics that made them unique and interesting people. This second session particularly focused on the importance of non-verbal communication. An explanation was given regarding how facial expression, posture, eye contact and gestures inform people of how we are feeling and how others are feeling too. This begins even before we start to talk to a person.

Activities

1   Warm-up: 'Getting to know you'
    Stand up and form a circle.

   (a) Throw the beanbag to a member of the group and call out your name as you throw it.
   (b) Throw the beanbag to a member of the group and call out his name.
   (c) Throw a beanbag to a member of the group and call out something you notice about the person, **i.e.** red jumper, gold watch, etc.

2   Body shapes
    This activity is used to help you appreciate your body's movement and how you can change its shape and position within an environment.

   (a) Make your body into a small shape.
   (b) Make your body into a fat shape.
   (c) Make your body into a thin shape.
   (d) Make your body into a round shape.
   (e) Make your body into a spiky shape.

3   Group organisation
    Line up according to your height with the tallest person at one end of the room and the shortest at the other, all members must see where they fit into the gradient but *no* verbal communication should be used. *This requires considerable eye contact and gesture.*
      Repeat the above exercise using hair colour; from darkest to lightest, age, house number, etc. (remember no verbal communication can be used).

4   Word organisation game
    The group is divided into two and a variety of letters are placed on cards or sticky-backed labels stuck on the top of each young person's feet and/or back of hands. The letters can be rearranged to make a number of words. The leader calls out a question and each group have to arrange their legs and hands to spell out the word, but no verbal communication is allowed.

    For example: if the letters 'HANDBAG' are placed on the top of the hand or feet questions could then be asked:

    (a) What is another name for a pop group?   BAND
    (b) What do you carry your shopping in?   BAG
    (c) What is another word for touch lightly?   DAB
    (d) What is located at the end of your arm?   HAND
    (e) What do ladies carry their purses in?   HANDBAG

This is fun activity which involves each group working cooperatively and placing hands and feet in all sorts of positions to format the word. It also requires each young person to work on balance and sequencing skills. The non-verbal element draws out a natural leader.

5   Emotions
    Each member of the group is given a card which describes an emotion, i.e. happy, frightened, worried. Each member expresses that emotion using non-verbal means, the rest of the group guess the emotion.

6   Charades
    The session concludes with a game of charades whereby each member of the group thinks about a famous film or TV programme and attempts to mime words connected with the title until it is guessed.

Conclude with group discussion and homework task.

- homework;
- put the sound off when watching a TV programme;
- see if you can work out how the characters are feeling by watching their non-verbal language. Jot down your ideas and bring these to the next group where they will be discussed.

Session 3: Observation

Session 3 commenced with a brief discussion regarding last week's observation of non-verbal cues on TV. This led onto a conversation stressing how eye contact and good observation skills are a fundamental aspect of building effective social relationships. The group were encouraged to discuss how they would feel if they met someone they knew only to be ignored. This session therefore focused on helping the young people to develop detailed observational skills.

- Walk around the room, greeting one another non-verbally. Do not touch or say anything. Use nods, bows, winks and other eye contact.
- Walk around the room, greeting one another. This time physical contact is allowed but no verbal communication, i.e. handshake, pat on the back, high five, etc.
- Walk around the room, greeting one another using verbal skills, i.e. hello, hi, good to see you, etc. and/or physical touch with eye contact.

Discuss how members managed to catch a person's attention.

1   Change three things about your appearance
     Members choose a partner and sit back to back without seeing each other, each
     member changes three things about his appearance, these can be overt such as
     having a jumper on back to front, or subtle such as placing a watch on another
     wrist. His partner must then guess what has been changed.

2   Frozen beanbag
     Each member is given a beanbag which they must balance on their head. The
     leader gives an instruction such as move forwards, backwards, faster, sideways,
     etc. If a beanbag falls off a young person's head they are frozen and must
     stand like a statue. This is a lovely game which requires observation, balance and
     postural control. They can all be released if someone observes their dilemma,
     reaches down to collect their beanbag while retaining their own on their head,
     and placing it back on their friend's head. The winner of the game is the one who
     helps the most people.

3   Winky murder
     The group concludes with a fun game of winky murder. One member of the
     group is allocated the role of detective and they leave the room and while they
     are outside the leader selects a person to be the 'murderer'. The murderer kills
     off his victims by winking at them. It is the detective's responsibility to observe
     who is committing the offences.

Following a discussion on the value of observation, homework was given, which
asked each young person to count how many times they greet people in a single day,
and to highlight any differences they notice in those they live with. For example, new
clothes, hair cut, etc.

Session 4: Spatial awareness and personal space

Session 4 commenced with a discussion on observations and whether members had
noticed anything different about the people they had got to know over the past week.
The session then introduced the theme for the week, stressing how important it is to
recognise that there is a respectable distance to keep when you are talking with
others, and how this differs according to whom you are speaking, i.e. whether it is
a relative, close friend or teacher. It was explained that this session would help to
develop spatial organisation and explore personal comfort in relation to proximity.

Activities

1   Warm-up. Close your eyes, what can you hear?

2   People-to-people game
     Choose a partner; stand together in a space in the room. Leader calls out
     instructions such as elbow to ear. The couple then have to negotiate how to
     connect one person's elbow to the other person's ear. This can progress in
     complexity depending on the physical skills you wish to challenge, for example
     a total of two feet only on the floor, requires considerable balance especially as
     the young people have motor coordination difficulties.

When the leader shouts 'people to people' everyone swaps partners. At the end of this game a discussion can ensue as to what individual positions people were comfortable with and those with which they were uncomfortable.

3   Describe a diagram
Working in pairs, members sit back to back. One of each pair is given a simple diagram. They must describe it to his partner who must reproduce it on a piece of paper. The challenge is to get the diagrams to look similar.

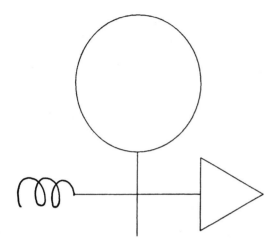

Figure 10.2 Example of a diagram to be described

This activity encourages verbal description but it also gives the leader an understanding of individual's form recognition and reproduction, along with his spatial planning and organisation.

4   Blind man's cross-over
One member of the group is blindfolded and stands in the middle of the room. Remaining members must try to sneak across the room without being caught. This activity involves controlled motor skills, planning a suitable pathway, and awareness of space and distance in relation to the central figure.

5   Breaking in and out of a circle
One member of the group remains on the periphery while the rest of the group hold hands and stand closely together to make a tightly knit circle, the external member must now try to get inside the circle using speed, strength and cunning. This can be repeated with a member trying to break out of the circle also. Discussion concludes the session as to how it felt being in such close proximity to each other and how it felt to be trapped inside or outside.

Homework involved observing how close people stand in relation to each other to communicate effectively. And answering the question: does the distance depend on their relationship to the person?

Session 5: Listening skills

Session 5 commenced with a short discussion regarding the group's observation of people's proximity. Following last week's homework, personal examples were shared relating to situations, which were comfortable and which were uncomfortable. This led to reiterating the importance of body language and non-verbal responses, which led to a discussion on how not only visual observation can help us understand how people are feeling, but how we must listen to what people are saying in order to develop a relationship with them.

The session emphasised that by listening to people we can then make an appropriate response to what they have said and shown. Listening and remembering is an essential skill if we want to form good relationships. Listening is far from a passive process. As listeners we can avoid speaking but we need to let the speaker know that we are following their conversation so they will continue to speak. We do this using good eye contact, non-verbal cues and occasional comments. If we do not encourage the speaker they may interpret our lack of interaction as disinterest.

Activities

1   Warm-up: introductions
    In pairs chat for one minute to your partner to find out a little about him, i.e., where he lives, favourite food, where he is going on holiday, which football team he supports, etc. Remember this information. Both partners have a turn.
    Draw the group back together. Each member must introduce their partner to the group sharing what they know about the person. This activity encourages both initiation of appropriate questions and listening skills.

2   Guess the voice
    One member of the group is blindfolded, and sits in the centre of a circle. The leader selects various members to say hello; the blindfolded young person must decide who has spoken. This activity encourages an awareness of variations in voice tone.

3   Chinese whispers
    The group sits in a circle and a poem, saying or rhyme is whispered to the first member of the group who must remember the expression and whisper it to the next person; this continues until the last person states the rhyme out loud. It has usually become quite distorted by the time it travels round the group, but the nearer it is to the original saying, the better the listening skills.

4   How are you feeling?
    One person leaves the room. Some of the remaining members are given a card with an emotion written or drawn on it, i.e. excited, angry, shy and nervous. These are then hidden. The person then returns to the group and must ask random questions to group members who must answer in the manner of their emotion. For example:

    Guesser: 'Did you have a good day at school today Mark?'
    Respondent: 'What is it to you? Mind your own businesses.'
    Emotion card: angry

This game encourages the initiation of questions and awareness of how voice tone can indicate different moods.

5   Adaptation of Mrs Brown went to town
Everyone sits in a circle; each member thinks of his favourite food. One person starts by stating their name and favourite food, the person next to them continues as follows: My name is Mark and I like spaghetti.
   His name is Mark, he likes spaghetti, my name is Peter and I like curry.
   His name is Mark, he likes spaghetti, his name is Peter and he likes curry, my name is Jack and I like pizza.
This continues so that each member is added, if the group are successful in recalling everyone's favourite food you can continue by adding dessert. This game encourages observation, good listening skills and a good sequential memory.

6   Book puzzles
Leader reads a chapter from a suitable book and at the end the group are split into two teams and must answer questions taken from the chapter to ascertain how well members have been listening.

7   Journalist
Two rows of chairs are formed at either side of the room with the backs of the chairs to the wall. The group is divided so that the young people on one side of the room are journalists, they have a clipboard and paper, the group on the opposite side are reporters, each has an extract from a newspaper, and each newspaper is different. Each reporter should have a journalist sitting opposite. When the leader calls start, each reporter must read out their headlines so that the journalist opposite can write it down, this is happening simultaneously so is quite noisy.
   The journalist who has the most words and has the most accurate reproduction of the headlines is the winner.

This game is great fun and develops auditory skills, in particular auditory figure–ground discrimination.
   Following this activity, discussion around listening in busy environments such as classrooms ensued. Homework was given to practise 'active' listening, for example to attend fully when a friend or member of your family converses; also the young people were encouraged to watch others when they were in conversation to determine whether they were good or bad listeners.

Session 6: Speaking skills

Session 6 commenced with a review of each young person's listening observations, this led onto an introduction of the session which focused on speaking skills. It emphasised that when we speak to others it is not only what we say that is important, but how we say it; and also to keep people interested in our conversation we need to adopt strategies to keep people's attention.

Activities

1   Warm-up
    Stand in a circle, throw the beanbag to members but call out something you
    know about them, i.e. hobby, where they are going on holiday, etc. This
    encourages recall, observation and listening skills.

2   Race commentator
    The leader selects a member of the group to recite a passage as fast as possible
    in the manner of a race commentator, the leader than asks the group questions
    to see how much was understood. Speed of conversation is then discussed.

3   Mouse-talking
    The leader selects a member of the group to recite a passage as quietly as possible
    in the manner of a mouse, and then asks the group questions to see how much
    was understood. Volume in conversation is then discussed.

4   Train loud-hailer
    The leader selects a member of the group to recite a passage as loud as possible
    in the manner of a train station loud-hailer; the leader then asks the group
    questions to see how much was understood. Volume of conversation is then
    further discussed.

5   Tortoise-talking
    The leader selects a member of the group to recite a passage as slowly as possible
    in the manner of a tortoise, the leader than asks the group questions to see how
    much was understood. Speed of conversation is then further discussed.

6   Conversational errors game
    A series of cards is made up with conversational errors written for example:
    interrupts conversations, poor eye contact, puts hand across mouth when
    talking, hesitates constantly etc. A pair is selected and given a few of these cards,
    they must hold a conversation incorporating these errors, the rest of the group
    must identify the errors. This is followed by a discussion on conversational
    etiquette.

Homework was given to listen to others having a conversation and to evaluate
whether they were following good rules of conversation.

Session 7: Personal qualities

Session 7 commenced with a review of the group's awareness of conversational
errors based on interactions they had either been involved in or where they had
listened to conversations and observed the interaction. This was followed by a
discussion regarding how we are all unique having differing abilities, talents and
interests. The fact that we are all different makes forming relationships so interesting.
Sometimes we might feel that we are not as able or interesting as another person is
but we must try to value our own skills and abilities rather than comparing ourselves
with others.

Activities

1   Each group member has to state three things that he is good at. This is often very difficult for children with dyspraxia but by this stage in the programme other group members were helping with suggestions.

2   Who is it?
     Each member writes a brief description of himself on a piece of paper, this is folded up and placed in the middle of the room in a bucket. Each member takes it in turns to draw a piece of paper, read it out and tries to guess who is described.

3   Confidence boost
     A person is placed in the middle of group. Remaining members sit in a circle around him. Each member must make positive comments about the person in the centre. Each member takes their turn to sit in the middle. This is such a positive game for self-esteem and confidence building.

4   Who in the group?
     The group members sit in a similar position to the previous game. One member starts by saying who in the group would you like to . . . Any event can be used but it must be positive, for example: who in the group would you like to take on holiday with you? Who in the group would you like to have a McDonald's meal with? Who in the group would you like to have near when you are ill?
         The central person must answer choosing members of the group. After a short time the question can be asked 'who in the group would you like to change places with?' and the central figure alters. This encourages feelings of affirmation plus initiation of questions.

5   Coat-of-arms
     Each young person is given a piece of paper with a shield drawn on it segmented into four quarters. Each young person has to draw or write the following information in each section:

     (a) Things I am good at.
     (b) Things I enjoy doing.
     (c) Places where I have had good fun.
     (d) Motto.

     The results are discussed with the group if desired.

For homework members were asked to think of an activity that they would love to do, but that they have been a little afraid to do because they might not be successful; it could be learning to play an instrument, or joining a club.
    They were then asked to write down a list of skills that are needed to help to achieve the goal. These should be shown to parents or teachers. They should be asked how they can help these goals to be realised.

Session 8: Teamwork

The final week was a great source of encouragement to the leader as many children came to the group informing others that they had done their homework and as a consequence had joined chess clubs, computer clubs, scouts and other activities set as part of individual goals. The final session stressed the importance of working as a team, and how this involves being able to take turns, listen to the ideas of others, ask questions, offer suggestions, and cooperate with others. It also explained that difficulties cooperating with others may seriously affect relationships.

Activities

1   Warm-up
    Who started the motion? The group sit in a circle, one member goes out of the room, a leader is selected who starts a rhythm such as a tap of the foot or clap or slap of a thigh, the rest of the group copy; when the chosen member returns to the group, the rhythm continues but changes every few minutes. The chosen member must decide who is changing the motion.
       This activity encourages group cooperation and acute observational skills as changes to the motion can be very subtle.

2   Spin the bottle
    The group sit in a circle on the floor, an empty beer bottle is spun in the middle; whoever spins the bottle must make a positive comment about the person it points to.

3   Famous people
    Each member of the group has a label placed on his back with the name of a famous person. Members move around the room asking their colleagues questions, i.e. am I a lady? Respondents can only answer yes or no. This continues until all famous people are guessed. This encourages the initiation of questions, careful listening and memory.

4   Body words
    The group is divided into half and each group has to think of a three- or four-letter word (depending on the numbers in their group). They must then form their bodies into the letters to see if the other group can guess the word.

5   Machines
    In similar-sized groups the young people have to invent a type of machine and work together to create it, presenting this to the other group. For example a bubble-making machine, a train, a washing machine. Both this exercise and 'body words' encourages group cooperation, team-building and body awareness.

The group concluded with a review of what each member felt they had learned and the completion of a self-esteem worksheet. The sheet used was taken by kind permission from the book, *Putting on the Brakes* by Quinn and Stern (1993) which, although written for children with attention deficit hyperactivity disorder (ADHD) has a considerable amount of valuable material which is appropriate for young people with dyspraxia.

MORE ABOUT ME

There are *many* things about you that make you SPECIAL. Here is a chance to "talk" about yourself.

Fill in these sentences so they describe you.

I am very good at _Computers_.

This year I have gotten better at _Self confidence_

My favorite subject at school is _Science_.

The subject I like least is _Geography_.

One of the best books I ever read was _Harry Potter Book 4_

If I could travel anywhere, I would like to go to _Japan_.

When I play with a friend, I like to _play computer games_

I like to _Go out and have fun_ with my family.

My favorite meal is ~~lamb casserole~~, and _Apple pie_

If I ~~could plan~~ the perfect day, this is what I would want ~~to do in the~~

morning _play computer games_

afternoon _go to the cinema_

evening _relax with my family_

Something about myself that I would like to change is _my speed eg not able to run fast_

What I like best about myself is _my consideration and kindness_

This page can also be shared with someone who is important to you.

Figure 10.3 Completed 'All-about-me' worksheet (Mark's)

Chapter 11

Practical support strategies

Many children will be expected to manage within the classroom without any additional resources provided by school. Some children with dyspraxia do qualify for and receive a Statement of Special Educational needs, but with the current targets of reducing the number of statements that are required (and issued) this is likely to become less common.

If a child with dyspraxia is seeing an occupational therapist or speech and language therapist, the therapist may provide a specific programme of exercises and support, which can be used at school and at home. These programmes, in addition to the child's Statement of Special Educational Needs, if he has one and/or an Individual Education Plan should inform practice.

Teachers and parents are often working under great pressure, and with this fact in mind we have decided to approach the area of support in two ways. First, we have offered subject-specific programmes, which relate directly to the National Curriculum, and so should make real sense to teachers in their work. We have then listed a number of general strategies, which can be introduced simply and with the minimum of fuss and which will really benefit the child with dyspraxia (and his peers).

We have intentionally incorporated the strategies for school and home within the same chapter, as it is impossible in reality to separate the two.

Science

There are other areas of the curriculum where children with dyspraxia may experience difficulties. One of these areas is science, which is a wonderfully exciting subject and has the potential to tap fully into a child's motivation to learn. However the curriculum does incorporate many practical experiments, it does require an appreciation of form, weight, size and measures, and it is beneficial to have an organized, logical mind in order to follow procedures and evaluate cause and effects. These are precisely the skills which the child with dyspraxia lacks.

The National Curriculum science programme covers four key study areas. Scientific enquiry, life processes and living things, materials and their properties and physical processes. Within these four areas it is expected that each pupil should reach the attainment target relevant to their level of study in:

1   Ideas and evidence.
2   Planning.

3   Carrying out.
4   Interpreting and evaluating.
5   Recording and presenting data.

If we consider some of the subject material covered under this programme we will see the potential concerns for children with dyspraxia.

Within the attainment target scientific enquiry, at the earliest level children are encouraged to 'describe or respond appropriately to simple features of objects, living things and events they observe, communicating their findings in simple ways for example, talking about their work, through drawings, simple charts'. Struggles in appreciating the three-dimensional qualities of objects can limit success in this.

We have already described some of the concerns that children with dyspraxia have in respect to recording ideas and ordering numerical data, which will affect science in a similar way. Also difficulties in estimation, measurement of depth and mass are all influenced by poor visual perception. The advantage of this subject is that subjective estimation is always balanced with an objective measure, thus helping the child to self-monitor his own abilities in approximation.

Teachers, however, must be aware that the instrumentation used in scientific enquiry must not be too complex and that simple solutions or measures can be used. Opportunities should be provided to use the computer to create graphs or tabulate results. Recording charts can be colour-coded to encourage children to place the figures in the appropriate columns.

In relation to attainment target 2, life processes and living things are relatively straightforward in the early stages requiring the child to name parts of the body, parts of plants, and animals and types of species, progressing onto developing knowledge regarding how living things live, i.e. food, growth, etc. appreciate life including growth and reproduction, and explore explanations for changes in living things. It is when the child reaches level 4 that difficulties will often occur as living systems are discussed and a relationship is found between systems. This will include body systems; how they connect and interact with one another, i.e. how the respiratory system links to the cardiovascular system. The child with dyspraxia may struggle to appreciate the connections between the body systems, be unable to perceive the size and position of organs within the human body. The difficulty in this area stems from the child's poor awareness of self and distorted form constancy, which affects judgment of size.

To address this it is beneficial to use anatomical models to describe bodily systems, rather than diagrams in books, and to utilise hands-on experiences such as those found in interactive museums and galleries such as Eureka and the Earth Centre (see the Appendix). This will develop a personal sense of proportion; provide segmenting lines which infer the approximate size of different proportions of the human body. This method can also be used when forming diagrams of other living things.

Attainment target 3 incorporates materials and their properties. This can be a problematic area of the science programme due to the child's poor sensory system and in particular tactile sensation. Within this target children are expected to identify a range of common materials and know about some of their properties. They also need to be able to describe similarities and differences between materials and explain how these differences are used to classify substances, for example as solids, liquids, gases, acids and alkalis. Processes such as filtration and distillation that are used to separate simple mixtures also figure at this level.

As the child's sense of tactile discrimination is diminished, they will rely heavily on other descriptors to appreciate the qualities of materials, in particular vision, verbal description, colour and shading. The child may attempt to sense receptors other than those in the hand, and may be seen putting materials to his lips, as this is the most sensitive area of the body. Processes will have to be explained practically rather than by using diagrams as retention of organised procedures is reinforced using demonstrable tasks.

Experiments in velocity may be a source of frustration as the child is unable to ascertain the exact weight of an object in relation to others. To help with estimation a simple set of scales can be used to help the child understand the velocity of materials.

The fourth attainment target, involving physical processes is possibly the most practically difficult target for children with dyspraxia to achieve, despite very good conceptual awareness of the procedures involved. Processes such as electricity, how a lightbulb works, pitch of sound, movement, speed and direction, motion, force and friction. The exciting practical experience involved in answering these questions often requires considerable dexterity. Consider wiring a plug or building a circuit and the size of the wires and preciseness of the soldering. These all require a degree of accuracy in placement and refined manipulation which the child with dyspraxia does not have. Enlarged models can help to alleviate this concern. In addition, visits to interactive science museums can be very rewarding.

There are several support networks which can offer advice regarding differentiation of science materials. In particular practical strategies set out in the National Curriculum Councils (1991 and 1992) and publications such as Booth *et al.* (2000) Copymaster can be very helpful. In addition associations such as Inclusive Science and Special Educational Needs (ISSEN), Access to Science Education (ASE) and the National Association for Special Educational Needs (NASEN) can all provide extremely useful and practical advice to ensure that science remains a dynamic and exciting subject for children of all abilities.

Art

The value of art in the National Curriculum has become increasingly acknowledged in relation to its emotional and expressive qualities. Art encourages children to express feelings, communicate using an alternative to speech and writing, and explore the varied sensory qualities of art materials. However, much art in school today is carried out on an ad hoc basis in relation to content and structure and remains a low priority in relation to the intense concerns for numeracy and literacy (Peter, 1996a).

As art is often seen as a subsidiary subject, the planning and systematic organisation of planned art and craft-based activities can be limited. It is widely acknowledged that it is the teacher of art that is the primary motivator for art appreciation. However this is another subject where confidence in one's own abilities may impact on how it is used in the classroom. As with maths, an acknowledgement of being poor at art is used to excuse efforts. Fear of ridicule from peers based on past experiences may still haunt those who feel that art is a gift which you either have or don't have. Consequently there is still the assumption that art must represent real-life objects. In actuality the National Curriculum focuses very little on naturalistic representations rather than emphasising the wonderful use of medium to create designs, patterns and textures. In addition children are encouraged to appreciate a variety of famous artists to observe how they have developed techniques which can be adopted today. Therefore it is important that each teacher puts aside his own concerns about his artistic ability to become an enabler, providing children with a range of medium and creative opportunities. It is also worth considering how personal concerns regarding artistic ability can be used positively to help children who may have a genuine reason for struggling with art and design.

Mary Peter's books (1996a, 1996b) are really useful guides to help children break down the various components required under the National Curriculum Art for All Policy. The attempts of children with dyspraxia at drawings and paintings may appear to be very immature and lack creativity, and it may be assumed that the child lacks imagination. This is not the case as the majority of children with dyspraxia have wonderful and varied ideas and simply need help to express these, taking into account their poor motor and perceptual ability.

Poor fine-motor coordination may impede a child's ability to control the tools and materials required to produce line and the intricacies of pattern. Struggles to control pressure through the upper limbs caused by poor proprioceptive feedback can cause pencil points to be easily broken, wax crayons snapped and charcoal crushed to dust! This needs to be considered when medium is given as simple alternatives can enable the child to proceed with their peers at a similar pace. For example use chubby wax crayons rather than fine crayons as these are more difficult to snap; use chubby chalks rather than fine pastels; use hard-leaded pencils rather than soft to reduce the need to sharpen them constantly or place the child's work on an easel so that the whole weight of the trunk is not transferred through the drawing tool thus increasing pressure. The use of an easel or blackboard only requires control of the upper limbs although lack of stability may impair control. If a child struggles to stabilise in a standing position, sit the child at an easel as this will stabilise the hip girdle so that the child can focus on controlling movements of the upper limbs.

The curriculum states that children should experiment with and appreciate a variety of forms of pattern. Children should learn to experiment with and use patterns in a range of media, add texture and develop this in both two and three dimensions. Again poorly developed hand–eye coordination can impair the child's ability to create linear patterns.

To help develop these skills pairing can help. Sit the child with a friend who will start with one line, the child then parallels this line in a similar colour to the best of his ability. A further line is drawn in another colour which again is paralleled with the help and guidance of their partner. This continues until a pattern is accomplished. Alternatively the use of simple tools and texture can also help. For example the use of thick paint with the addition of concentrated washing up liquid can be spread over a piece of card and patterns can be formed using a wide-toothed comb, a fork or fingers.

The early introduction to great artists of the Impressionist era can demonstrate how art does not have to use pencil or paintbrush in precise strokes but can demonstrate how combinations of colour simply placed on paper can have an impressive effect.

The appreciation of texture plays a large part in the art curriculum. 'Developing a sense of touch and awareness that everything around them has its own texture is an integral part of pupils' sensory exploration and discovery of their world and how materials behave' (Peter, 1996b, p. 24). Children need hands-on experiences of a range of textures as a foundation on which to develop artistic expression. In order to appreciate a range of textures children need to have adequate sensory feedback and in particular tactile sensation. We know that the majority of children with dyspraxia have either diminished sensation or overresponsive sensation, which will have repercussions when exploring different textures. For those with diminished sensation, the subtleties of textual changes may be difficult to appreciate. To understand this, consider the task of washing-up. Often rubber gloves are worn to protect the hands from detergent and high temperature. By wearing gloves, sensation is diminished; it is possible to identify and clean large items of food stuck onto a dish, but it becomes more problematic when smaller items remain. Also you will note that dexterity deteriorates when tactile sensation is diminished. This is a similar scenario for children with dyspraxia as precise sensation is lacking. This can be helped by using more pronounced textures rather than subtle changes in materials, for example use course sand mixed with paint to create texture, use thick string to form patterns rather than wool or fine string, add soda crystals to paint to thicken texture rather than poster paints.

We have previously mentioned children who are what is known as 'tactile defensive', which is a condition in which an individual can be extremely sensitive to light touch. Theoretically, when the tactile system is immature and working improperly, abnormal neural signals are sent to the cortex in the brain which can interfere with other brain processes. This in turn causes the brain to be overly stimulated and may lead to excessive brain activity, which can neither be turned off nor organized (Hatch-Rasmussen, 1995). Children who are tactile defensive find many textures *too* stimulating; these are children who always seem to be taking their jumpers off come rain or shine because 'it itches!'. This overt sensitivity may cause children to be intensely uncomfortable when exploring textures and therefore it is important to ascertain which textures are more acceptable than others. This requires the child to have opportunities to explore a variety of textures in a safe setting such as in a small group. It is impossible to list acceptable medium, as each child is uniquely different. The key is to allow opportunities for exploration and observe the child's preferences, noting these to build on future skills.

Many children who are tactile defensive benefit from slow movements which encourage deep pressure through the upper limbs, therefore activities which for example may involve pressing down through clay, and heavy printing tasks may be more comfortable. A further area of art which is explored in depth throughout the child's education is the use of colour. Colour should be introduced slowly and gradually as the huge array of variations can indeed appear overwhelming. Children are taught colour combinations and how colours can represent temperatures. It is important that colour is also taught in terms of harmonising colour versus discordant colour. This is an area where many children with dyspraxia struggle and it is demonstrated in their choice of clothing. As subtle variations in tone are often not recognised by the child with dyspraxia, colour combinations can frequently clash, as one young college student with dyspraxia informed me.

> 'You can *see* me before you meet me, because I have usually got my clothing colour combination all wrong! I usually end up combining certain shades of orange with scarlet. Rather than get bugged by comments I tell everyone it's a fashion statement!'

In addition to recognising colour variations, children are also expected to explore different dimensions using line and tone. In order to be able to experiment with tone they must appreciate contrasts in lighting. These subtleties again can be lacking in children with dyspraxia and they may need help to present tonal changes. If a child struggles with pressure through the upper limbs, the drawing medium can be used to demonstrate tonal changes rather than pressure through the pencil. Soft-leaded pencils such as B and 2B can be used to demonstrate darker tone while harder lead such as HB can be used for lighter shades.

As controlling media to produce tonal changes is particularly challenging, especially to shade with different degrees of intensity, it is worth considering lowering the height of the work surface.

When using line and tone to recreate naturalistic images, the child will need to select and edit potential images to reproduce, be this a still-life display, an individual or scene. If an outdoor scene is chosen the child with visual figure–ground discrimination difficulties will struggle with a barrage of potential images and may find it difficult to select that which has most significance to them. To help alleviate this concern a screen or picture mount, or opened box can be used to narrow the visual field and help the child to select a specific area to sketch.

In attempting still-life drawings, the use of photographs can make sketching easier than synthesising impressions of real-life scenarios. The image can be created at a child's own pace without the pressure of the object being moved or altered. The introduction to famous artists who used more abstract methods of recreating naturalistic forms can help considerably at this stage when the child may be anxious to reproduce an image in its truest form.

There is considerable emphasis on shape, form and space in the art curriculum with children being encouraged to use these elements creatively and also to explore these in relation to one another. In addition, 'Pupils should be offered opportunities to reflect their growing understanding and knowledge of shape, form and space, in both two and three-dimensional art-making experiences (Peter, 1996b, p. 53). As children with dyspraxia struggle to understand the nuances of shape and form and particularly struggle with spatial relationships, this is reflected in their art. To help the child to appreciate form and shape multi-sensory experiences are needed.

The curriculum also expects children to develop an appreciation of a variety of materials. Extreme examples should be given to the child in order to help contrast differences, for example, brick with cotton wool, clay with silk, etc.

Perspective and proportions are a further aspect of the curriculum which will be affected by poor assessment of depth and confusion in size differentiation. This can be clearly seen in self-drawings where proportions are erratic making the image appear very immature.

It is worth simultaneously introducing the child to a series of famous artists who used and distorted perspective to create unique images, e.g. Picasso and Lowry. The appreciation of abstract art can be very liberating for children who struggle with visual perception.

There is evidence that movement, dance, music, experience of a variety of medium can all help the child to be successful in this aspect of the curriculum. Schoemaker (1993) used sensorimotor training techniques which included static and dynamic balance, work against resistance to ascertain the benefits to a child's ability to draw. The results were significant; in particular components of drawing such as movement, time, fluency and pause duration were dramatically improved.

Thoughtful use of computer-aided art and design processes will also enhance art-making opportunities. *Art in the National Curriculum* (DFE 1995) requires only that 'pupils should be given the opportunities where appropriate, to develop and apply their IT capability in their study of art, craft and design' (p. 1).

According to Winser (1996) time should be allocated to teach pupils those aspects of the use of IT which will:

- develop their visual perception;
- develop their creative and practical skills;
- extend their imaginative capability;
- enable them to express their feelings and ideas.

(Cited in Peter, 1996b, p. 67)

The use of IT in art is particularly helpful in:

- generating patterns to help in design;
- colour matching and mixing;
- modifying line, shape and tone;
- assisting with the three-dimensional qualities of design.

However, it is important to be aware that some software is complex to use and can be visually cluttered.

It is hoped that the suggestions provided will enable children to respond to and appreciate art, craft and design; to develop into confident users of a variety of creative medium to produce with imagination pieces of work to be proud of.

Literacy

There has been an increasing emphasis on improving children's literacy over the past five years in order to encourage speaking, listening, group discussion and inter-action, drama, use of English, language variation, reading and writing. The National Literacy Strategy (NLS) recommends a framework of pre-specified objectives for each term's teaching in word, sentence and text-level work. This involves dedicated teaching time with the following framework being recommended:

- Shared reading and writing with the whole class (15 minutes), concentrating on aspects of text selected from the framework of objectives, e.g. looking at story settings.
- Structured grammar and phonic work with the whole class (15 minutes), e.g. to search for, identify and classify a range of prepositions, usually using the text from the first part of the hour.
- Twenty minutes during which the teacher works with a group (or two groups in Key Stage 1) of children in a differentiated group of six to eight pupils, on guided reading or writing with the teacher and the rest of the class work independently, e.g. practising skills covered earlier.
- A 10-minute plenary with the whole class, reviewing what they have learned.

On the whole teachers have continued to follow this structure. However, there are certain aspects of the NLS and particularly this structure which may impact on the child with dyspraxia.

During the initial whole-class section teachers often use 'big books' to help children to appreciate the context, language structure and grammar involved in composition. Children are usually seated on the floor, surrounding the teacher. In this position, children with visual figure–ground discrimination difficulties may easily become distracted by the close proximity of the group and range of information within his visual field, thus the child may struggle to attend and observe. To alleviate this, the child should be seated directly in front of the teacher so that attention can be maintained. Alternatively the child can be given his own smaller copy of the book to follow.

When the child is introduced to letter shapes, confusion may arise due to poor form constancy. It is therefore important that multi-sensory methods are utilised to help the child recognise letterforms and demonstrate how they connect together to make words.

The child with motor dyspraxia (not verbal dyspraxia) will often thrive in discussions pertaining to introduced texts and reading ability will initially develop well. However, as the child proceeds through Key Stage 1 deterioration in reading may be noted. This is not due to a cognitive deficiency but perceptual acuity. The increase in volume of information on a page and decrease in font size will cause those with figure–ground discrimination difficulties to struggle. There are several ways this can be addressed: writing font can be enlarged, a reading window can be provided, supporting illustrations can be separated from the text, the text can be reproduced in a clearer font or cursive style, and coloured overlays can be used to soften the contrast between black print on a white surface. It is very important that the child is not offered a younger-aged reading book simply because the font is clearer.

Children who struggle with spelling because of poor visual closure may be helped if the spelling is demonstrated in cursive form; this enables the child to visually remember the word as a whole unit rather than a sequence of separate letters. Visual closure is the ability to perceive wholes out of parts. How to help children spell begs the question whether we spell by eye, ear or hand (Westwood, 1997). It is almost certain that we use all three modalities, that is visual information, phonemic awareness and kinaesthetic feedback to help reinforce the structure of words. 'A Hand for

Spelling' by Charles Cripps and the Finger Phonics by Lloyd, Wernham and Jolly are constructive in encouraging all three modalities.

Auditory perception has a bearing on learning to read (Pressley and McCormick, 1995). The acquisition of phonic skills is dependent upon phonetic awareness but children with developmental verbal dyspraxia (DVD) will struggle to sound out letter forms and this may influence their phonetic distinction, therefore they may confuse words such as 'bear' and 'pear'. Classroom games can be used to help the child distinguish words according to their sounds, spelling and image.

Successful reading also requires auditory analysis or segmentation; this involves the ability to isolate individual sounds in a word. Again children with DVD will struggle with this because of poor expressive language. Phoneme blending is also an issue for those who struggle to sound out letters. TV programmes such as the BBC's *Words and Pictures Plus* is particularly useful in helping children to analyse letter sounds and blends. In addition, the use of a word processor for story creation can assist in the development of phonic analysis and segmentation (Westwood, 1997).

During individual reading the use of an angled board will help to maintain the child's visual focus. The angled board helps the child to focus and attend to the text. As an alternative a reading screen can be made easily. These are foldable screens made from a light MDF or plywood material which can be used to surround the child when reading. All class members will benefit from these simple screens, not just the child with dyspraxia.

When a child is working on paired reading with a partner it is important that the child is positioned in a way that he can scan effectively and that the book is placed appropriately. Ideally the book should be placed on an angled board.

Children with dyspraxia may have difficulties in reading *silently* owing to their need for multiple sensory reinforcement, in which case the child may be heard mumbling the text to himself. This can be irritating to his peers. The allocation of a quiet reading area may help or use of reading screens can help in this situation.

Children with DVD may become extremely distressed if expected to read out loud, even if this is one to one with the teacher. It may therefore be difficult to assess the child's understanding and comprehension of the material. To help with this provide a series of responses to a selected book, either in word or picture form depending on the age of the child. A quiz can then be given and the words or pictures can be selected by the child in response to the questions.

Writing composition may be severely restricted by poor handwriting. This can be incredibly frustrating for a child who has lots of ideas and a wonderful creative imagination, but who cannot control the pencil to write these down in a legible format. Alternative means of documentation should be sought to provide a quick and efficient means of recording ideas. Children with DVD in addition to motor dyspraxia will have further problems in expressing their ideas, and creative ways are needed to help the child unfold his ideas, this can involve using cartoon drawings to express ideas, computer graphics, collages, and the construction of story boards using comic and magazine cuttings.

Most of the techniques and adaptations recommended will help children with dyspraxia to develop their literacy skills and can be practically accommodated within the classroom with some forethought and planning on the teacher's behalf.

Liaison with the speech and language therapist as to the best approaches to use for children with DVD can ensure that they are not disadvantaged.

General strategies

The following list may prove helpful.

- Give an honest acknowledgement of a child's difficulties. The importance of this cannot be stressed enough. Sensitively sharing with others, including peers, that the difficulties experienced are not due to lack of motivation, ability or effort. How can people be supportive if they do not know that there is anything that needs supporting? Many people will quote how cruel children can be when it comes to dealing with someone who is 'different'. Conversely, children are usually very matter of fact about information relating to special needs if they are given the chance to share and discuss it. If inclusion is to stand any chance at all, it should start in the early years. Allow other children the opportunity to learn about dyspraxia, and to consider how they would feel if they were a child with dyspraxia. Allow children and staff to ask questions and expand their knowledge. Be positive in your approach and attitude, and make them feel important in the part they have to play in this child's success or failure.
- Teaching children relaxation exercises may help them through the day. Breath control may minimise anxiety, or anger born of frustration *and* may enhance general self-control. Ask the child to take a long slow deep breath and to exhale slowly too. Some children find that visualising something restful or pleasant can be helpful. Teaching a child that it is OK to say 'please give me a minute' when asked a question, thus allowing them to consider and formulate a reply.
- Explore useful adaptations. For example, embrace Velcro at every opportunity, use wet wipes instead of dry toilet paper for ease of cleansing, and allow the child to use a computer instead of writing. Rubber matting under equipment to stabilise it can be helpful.
- Take short-cuts if they relieve stress. It may be unrealistic for a family to expect their child to get dressed efficiently in a hurry before school. Such times are usually high in pressure, and parents should agree a plan that makes such times as easy as possible for everyone (e.g. they may agree to help the child with dressing on school mornings).
- Give more time. Children with dyspraxia need extra time to start work, to plan what they are going to do and to complete it. They may need more time to respond to questions. Allow them to have copies of your notes, or why not use a tape recorder to record the lesson, thus alleviating some of the pressure imposed by lack of time?
- Have a memo board at home, near to the exit. Any last minute changes or requirements can be chalked on this so that everyone remembers.
- Praise effort rather than achievement. If prizes were given purely for effort it is fair to say that a child with dyspraxia would have a cupboard full of shiny cups.
- Talk to the child. Ask him what you might do better. These children often employ wonderful strategies to assist their performance at school and in the home. It is important to be flexible and not see these as short-cuts, but as an effective means to an end.

- Try to incorporate 'learning breaks' to improve retention, i.e. switch tasks two to three times during the session.
- Ensure that instructions are given clearly and simply. Avoid long strings of instructions, which will leave the child with dyspraxia confused and vulnerable. Teachers may like to 'test' themselves on this by taking a tape recorder into a session that they are teaching. It is surprising how complex instructions can be when we listen to ourselves giving them!
- Do not show frustration. Remembering that if you are frustrated that the pupil cannot do something it is likely to be much worse for the pupil. It can be especially frustrating when a child with dyspraxia cannot do something today that they were able to do yesterday. Try to remain calm and express confidence that together you will eventually succeed.
- Encourage the child to compete against himself. Do not expect them to compete against others or some ideal or average target. Use an egg timer or similar timing device to improve upon a previous target.
- Discreetly watch playground experiences – allow the child to come into school (with one or two others) if there is a threat of bullying, or if the pupil finds the playground space and noise daunting. A quiet area or buddy scheme may be helpful.
- Have available an adult-led game in the playground where children then have the choice to join in.
- Allow a home/school diary. This is not a 'naughty book' and does not need to be written in each and every day. It is though an avenue for communication between parents and schools and fosters a healthy partnership between these equally important areas of a child's development.
- Practise physical skills in different situations. Break down complex skills into smaller and simpler parts, being aware that some activities we take for granted (e.g. carrying a dinner tray) may be complex for the pupil.
- Do not expect the pupil to listen and do simultaneously – e.g. avoiding listening/watching and taking notes at the same time.
- Seat the pupil sensitively. He should be able to see/listen without constant twisting and turning.
- Monitor the language used to the child – minimising the use of phrases like, 'You're so slow to finish'; 'You are last again', 'Can't you sit still?' 'You managed to do it before'.
- Provide shorter tasks, especially for homework. Avoid constant reminders to the pupil to hurry up or to work faster (this makes matters worse).
- Avoid offering rewards for better behaviour. When the pupil lacks the skills and planning to achieve the behaviour or the ability to ignore distractions this can become a very negative strategy.
- Ensure that the classroom equipment is well organised and easily accessible. Colour-coding of materials, ensuring there are clear classroom routines, and minimising changes can make a great deal of difference.
- Provide structures and steps in tasks. Try highlighting key words in texts used for reference, providing 'templates' for written work to prompt appropriate layout. Increase use of computer for written work for children with writing and presentation difficulties.

- Keep copying and redrafting to a minimum. Especially copying from the whiteboard.
- Remember that the pupil may tire more quickly. Working much harder than others because of level of concentration needed is tiring. Try to provide breaks in activities.
- Provide a range of strategies to support organisation. Colour-coding, forward planning, the use of technology. For a child in secondary school it is often useful to have a separate clear folder for every subject, in which the essentials (pen, pencil, ruler, rubber, etc.) can be placed. The child will then always arrive in class prepared.
- Homework may be helped by alternative recording styles. Setting shorter tasks, agreeing with the pupil and parents a reasonable amount of time the child should spend each day on homework (and tailoring the tasks set so this time limit is realistic).
- Offer a homework club – to allow extra time/help for those that need it.
- Mark written work on content, not presentation.
- Give thought to clothing. Clothes which minimise difficulties with dressing.
- Structure the approach to teaching. Learning should be multi-sensory and multi-cue.
- Employ a 'secret contract'. Many children with specific learning difficulties learn little in class because they are stressed. They may fear being asked a question and looking a fool, being asked to read out loud, not understanding what is being taught. It can be very useful to remove that stress by discreetly agreeing with the child that you will stand in a certain place or position, which will act as a cue to them, that you are going to ask them a question. This gives them time to think and compose themselves. Then ensure that they understand that they will be able to answer it! You have removed the stress and the child can now concentrate on learning the subject.
- Check that the pupil understands the language used. Keep instructions simple and single, avoiding long strings of instructions. It may be worth asking parents to introduce any new vocabulary that is likely to be used that week.
- Where necessary, encourage the child to use signs and gestures to reinforce communication.
- Teach the child to watch the face of the person talking. This will help the child with developmental verbal dyspraxia to imitate lip movements and facial expressions.
- Teach the child good listening skills. Support listening with visual cues and gain the child's attention before speaking.
- For children who have communication difficulties, acknowledge these honestly – 'it's difficult, but you're good at trying'. Avoid correction or comment in front of others in the class.
- Give an overview or context for the day's lesson as this enables the child to attempt some planning and assess how much effort is required during each part of the day.
- Use pauses to allow information to be processed and allow time for responses.
- Review what has been covered in the session. Reinforce learning by briefly summarising the lesson's outcomes.

- Write key vocabulary on the board as this will not only act as a prompt to help organisation, but will also help the child with communication difficulties to have a physical prompt from which to demonstrate his knowledge.
- Give visual backup when explaining new words. These can be in picture form, gesture or action.

For children with developmental verbal dyspraxia further advice can be sought from the speech and language therapist. Detailed targets and strategies may be given according to the child's specific requirements. This information will be used to inform the child's Individual Education Plan (IEP) and if targets are set collaboratively between the speech and language therapist and teacher success will be realistic and attainable. In addition to the suggestions described, the speech and language therapist may use a variety of programmes to facilitate the development of the child's speech system. These include:

- The Nuffield Dyspraxia Programme – aimed at improving the 'motor programming' of the child. It combines oral skills work with sound production and sequencing.
- Metaphon – a programme aimed at increasing the child's awareness of the features of sounds, e.g. noisy/quiet (voiced/voiceless sounds).
- Signing – this may be taught as a means of supporting verbal communication.
- Cued articulation – a set of pictures to represent a particular sound to aid production.

The speech and language therapist will explain the methods and programmes they will introduce in more detail.

One of the most important ways in which you can help the child with dyspraxia is to provide activities which are age appropriate, achievable and most of all *fun*! The following ideas embrace activities which can be incorporated into fun playtime and are the kind of things that all children will enjoy doing. So, these can be used with a small group or whole family. Fun and laughter are very motivating and the child is likely to return for more if he has enjoyed himself.

- Time yourself picking up cottonwool balls with tweezers.
- Pick up matches or cocktail sticks one by one, keeping them in your hand as you pick another up!
- Cut out shapes with scissors, make snowflakes at Christmas and paper chains for other occasions.
- Stand up/knock down dominoes. Increase the number you can balance.
- Roll out plasticine or play dough into the thinnest possible sausage, create letter shapes with these.
- Thread a lace in and out of holes in a card.
- Thread beads.
- Trace around pictures from a comic or magazine, make a scrapbook with samples.
- Dot-to-dot pictures.
- Sort objects (i.e. mix up matches, beads, paperclips, etc. and ask the child to sort them out).

- Play with finger puppets.
- Use appropriate nursery rhymes (Peter Pointer, One, two, three, four, five . . .).
- Spray the houseplants (or each other) with a plant sprayer. They are also great fun in the bath. Alternatively use 'crazy soap' – squirty bath soap!
- Blow and suck through different pipes, tubes, straws, etc. Use twirly straws at break times.
- Make funny faces in a mirror.
- Play licking games: lollies, cooking spoons, sugar off lips. This helps to develop oral control and helps with body awareness.
- Blow bubbles, blow paints, blow recorders, whistles, etc.
- Sing together adding actions when appropriate.
- Use different voices in role-play games and with different volumes.
- Breath control. Holding notes, using a blowpipe and ball, or play blow football.
- Play games which involve controlled finger flicking, i.e. Subbuteo, Hungry Hippos.
- Tape a favourite TV programme and then watch it with no volume. Guess what might be happening by the body language and other clues.

It is often difficult for parents and teachers to justify seemingly trivial activities when the child has such complex problems, and there may be a certain amount of concern that free time should be spent 'working' on aspects of handwriting, maths and gross motor skills, but, be assured, these activities should be fully embraced as they are not only developing the child's fine-motor skills, but are enabling the child to have fun and relax, appreciating the importance of 'being' and playing. After all children with dyspraxia are human beings not human doings!

Chapter 12

From confusion to inclusion

It is important to appreciate that changes in placement really have taken place for children with special needs. It may well be that there is a long way to go before we are truly inclusive, but times have changed. It is now the concept of 'special' that we need to change in order that we can stop drawing a line between what is considered 'normal' and what is not.

Because of our very practical experience of working and living with children with dyspraxia we are aware of the notion that, while this is all very well in theory, can it really fit into the real world, of busy teachers with big classes and few staff? We are also aware that we hear of the negative educational experiences all too often and so we thought it would be nice to include some very real classroom/school experiences, which are both positive and effective.

Putting theory into practice

Mr Richards says:

Joseph was always very disruptive after PE when it came to getting dressed. Because he found dressing difficult and the noise and movement of others so distracting, he always resorted to playing the fool and being generally excitable and uncooperative. He continually received negative feedback from both the staff and other pupils and he began to dread PE sessions as a consequence of this. The staff decided to give him his own area for dressing and he was able to use a cubicle on his own where he could concentrate on the task in hand. The difference this made was unbelievable. Joseph dressed well and was certainly not the last to be ready. Such a simple strategy made a huge difference.

Mrs Ashworth says:

Billie was always fidgeting; he seemed genuinely unable to sit still for any length of time. I decided to use him as the person to run errands or to gather equipment. Any message that needed to be run, Billie was the boy to do it and this enabled him to exercise often and in a meaningful way. I also invited the whole class to do a few exercises at regular intervals and found that this improved everybody's concentration.

Mr Bolton says:

The wee lad just couldn't cross his legs at storytime. I remember asking myself why I asked the children to cross their legs and decided that it was to make them look 'tidy' to others who may be passing and it looked like I was in control. I decided to get some carpet squares and at storytime all the children grabbed their square and sat comfortably on it. The wee boy with dyspraxia was given a little more legroom, and suddenly he really began to listen. The group may not have looked particularly tidy but goodness me they gained a great deal more from the session than they had done previously.

Mrs Lee says:

I can remember reading the list that the speech and language therapist sent to school about exercises to strengthen facial muscles. It looked time-consuming but one strategy we chose to employ was to buy each child one of those straws with all the twists and turns in them. All the children sucked through them at lunchtime and Danielle benefited from some exercises at the same time.

Mrs Hoad says:

How about a secondary school which let a football-mad 15-year-old play on both sides at once because he could never work out which way his side was going. Whatever he did was right for one side and the other kids tolerated this as he was seen as an 'extra' and they understood his difficulties.

Sue says:

Peter, who has dyspraxia, has been allowed to use a laptop at school in all lessons. His keyboarding skills are good and at a recent review of laptop usage in the school, he was the only one whose work rate has increased since he has been using this alternative to handwriting. Excellent stuff.

Mrs Pearcy says:

Joe's speech was pretty unintelligible and this was a great hardship to him at school. He was always desperate to tell me what he had done at the weekend, and I would struggle to understand. The use of a home/school diary really helped with this situation. Mum would write what had happened and I would read it without Joe seeing. Then when he told me what he had done I could have a really good stab at understanding him. He simply glowed with his achievement.

Mrs Clark says:

The use of visual symbols is really helpful for a lot of children with a variety of learning difficulties. They can mean the difference between understanding and a degree of independence and being totally lost and dependent.

Patrick

Patrick is a 10-year-old boy with dyspraxia who cannot sit still for long periods of time, and this has become an issue at certain times of the day when other children in the class are trying to concentrate and pay attention. His teacher brought a large beanbag cushion into class and Patrick is invited to sit on that at these times, and is given some space in which to move without disrupting others.

This has allowed him to be included in the activities without disrupting others.

These stories show that understanding, flexibility and empathy for the child really do work. Children who may have become troublesome and possibly eventually disaffected are instead catered for and truly included in mainstream education. It is hoped that a positive school experience and a feeling of belonging is something that they can carry with them into their adult life and enable them and those around them to be part of a society in which they both belong and can enrich.

A final story

An 8-year-old boy who was known to have dyspraxia wanted to use the toilet during a school playtime. He knew he was slow to dress and undress, he felt insecure with his feet dangling down from the toilet, and he had real difficulties cleansing himself when he had finished.

Fortunately he was at a school where the staff were both caring and flexible. When he had entered the school the staff had met with his parents and discussed the kind of difficulties young Matthew faced. Toileting had been highlighted as something that caused the little boy great anxiety and the parents were trying to educate him to use the toilet at home before going to school. However, the school had a toilet facility for those with disabilities and Matthew was offered the use of that. To ensure he felt comfortable the staff had also offered him the use of the staff toilet, which was located in the corridor close to his classroom. Both facilities had been fitted with handrails and the staff had placed a footstool in each toilet so that Matthew would feel secure when seated. His mother had supplied some moist toilet tissue and ensured his trousers were those with an elasticised waist that were easy to get both off and on. A mirror had been placed on the wall, to enable Matthew to check his clothing after using the toilet.

Matthew could slip into the toilet almost unnoticed and using the toilet was not something he dreaded anymore. In fact because this experience was made as easy as possible for him, and the school had made all kinds of minor changes to the environment and class work, Matthew really felt much like anyone else.

His peers were supportive, because the teacher had talked about dyspraxia with them all, and they had a real understanding of Matthew's difficulties and needs. She was pleasantly surprised by their interest and by the difference it made to the way Matthew had been accepted into class.

Matthew's parents were delighted and went to work knowing that Matthew was in an environment that was suited to his needs, with staff who were flexible and really keen to include Matthew fully into the school curriculum. The teachers were delighted by the way Matthew was working and they reflected on how much they had learned from him and his parents.

Matthew really enjoyed school and was happy to go knowing that he was able to succeed in all manner of personal and educational efforts. He felt that he belonged.

We sincerely hope that having read this book you will now realise that dyspraxia is indeed a very complex and far-reaching disability. Far from being uncooperative and often puzzling these children are in fact incredible. They are often working in a system that doesn't truly accommodate their needs and they function on the whole magnificently in a very confusing world. You may well be one of those who has been totally confused and exasperated by children with dyspraxia, but we trust that your understanding will now allow you to include and support these children in your mainstream classrooms.

We truly hope that we have taken you on a journey from confusion to inclusion.

Appendix: Useful addresses and recommended programmes

AbilityNet
Tel: 0800 269545
http://www.AbilityNet.org.uk

Advisory Centre for Education
Unit1C
Aberdeen Studios
22 Highbury Grove
London N5 2EA
Tel: 0800 800 5793
www.ace-ed.org.uk
An independent organisation offering advice relating to state education in England and Wales.

AFASIC (Association for all Speech-Impaired Children)
2nd Floor
50–2 Great Sutton Street
London EC1V ODJ
Tel: 020 7490 9410
Helpline: 08453 555577
www.afasic.org.uk
Offers help, information and advice for children and families who have children with speech and language impairments.

Bullying advice and information
Tel: 020 7378 1446
www.bullying.co.uk/
Advice, information and links relating to bullying.

Callirobics™ by Liora Laufer
PO Box 6634
Charlottesville, VA 22906
1-800-769-2891
Fax 1-434-293-9008

Contact a Family
209–11 City Road
London EC1V 1JN
Tel: 020 7608 8700
www.cafamily.org.uk
A charity that helps families and carers of children with SEN.

CSIE (Centre for Studies on Inclusive Education)
Room 2S, 203
S Block
Frenchay Campus
Coldharbour Lane
Bristol BS16 1QU
Tel: 0117 344 4007
www.inclusion.org.uk
Research and information relating to inclusion.

Cuisinaire
11 Crown Street
Reading RG1 2TQ

Department for Education and Skills
Sanctuary Buildings
Great Smith Street
London SW1P 3BT
Tel: 0870 000 2288
www.dfes.gov.uk

DfES Publications Centre
PO Box 5050
Sherwood park
Annesley
Nottingham NG15 0DJ
Tel: 0845 60 22 60
E-mail: dfes@prolog.uk.com
For an excellent range of books and
information relating to SEN and
education.

Disability Equality in Education
Unit 4Q
Leroy House
436 Essex Road
London N1 3QP
Tel: 020 7359 2855
www.diseed.org.uk/
Information, training and advice
relating to disability and equality issues
in education.

Dyspraxia Foundation
8 West Alley
Hitchin
Herts SG5 1EG
Tel: 01462 455016
Helpline: 01462 454986
www.dyspraxiafoundation.org.uk
For information, advice and contact
information of local support group
network.

The Earth Centre
Denaby Main
Doncaster DN12 4EA
Tel: 01709 513939
www.earthcentre.org.uk

Education Otherwise
PO Box 7420
London N9 9SG
Tel: 0870 7300074
www.education-otherwise.org/
For information and advice relating to
educating children at home.

Eureka Children's Museum
Discovery Road
Halifax HX1 2NE
www.eureka.org.uk

**The Fairley House Touch Typing
Program**
IEC Software
77 Orton Drive
Womborne
South Staffordshire WV5 9AP

Finger Phonics/Jolly Phonics
By Lloyd, Wernham and Jolly
Formative Fun Stores and many Early
Learning Centre outlets

Grippit 2000
Saracen Products Ltd
211 Saracen Street
Glasgow G22 5JN
www.grippit2000.com

Handhuggers
Sanford UK
Oldmeadow Road
King's Lynn
Norfolk PE30 4JR
Tel: 01553 761221

**Handprints: Home Program for Hand
Skills**™
Imaginart
PRO-Ed Inc
8700 Shoal Creek Boulevard
Austin
Texas
E-mail: feedback@proedinc.com

Handwriting for Windows™
KBER Kath Balcombe (Educational
Resources) Little Tudor
50 Kennedy Road
Shrewsbury SY3 7AA
Tel: 01743 340062
E-mail: kath@kber.co.uk

Handwriting without Tears™
By Jan Z. Olsen
The Psychological Corporation
Freepost WD147
Harcourt Place
32 Jamestown Road
London NW1 1YA

Happy Puzzle Company
PO Box 24041
London NW4 2ZN
Tel: 0800 376 3727
www.happypuzzle.co.uk/
Sells an exciting range of games and
puzzles to assist in strengthening areas
of weakness in children with a variety
of SEN, including dyspraxia.

ICAN
4 Dyers Buildings
Holborn
London EC1N 2QP
Tel: 0870 0104066
www.ican.org.uk
Specialises in the education of children
with speech and language
impairments.

In-hand manipulation ideas
www3.sympatico.ca/lansdowne.
children

**IPSEA (Independent Panel for Special
Educational Advice)**
6 Carlow Mews
Woodbridge
Suffolk IP12 1EA
Tel: 01394 380518
Helpline: 0800 0184106
www.ipsea.org.uk
Advice and support for issues relating
to SEN.

JABADAO
Branch House
18 Branch Road
Armley
Leeds LS12 3AO
Tel: 0113 231 0650
www.jabadao.org/
Offers training and courses relating to
movement in the early years.

LDA
Duke Street
Wisbech
Cambs PE13 2AE
Tel: 01945 463441
Produces the following programmes:
• A Hand for Spelling by Charles
  Cripps
• Activities for Geometric Solids
• Bucket Balance
• Creepy Crawlers
• Fraction Dominoes
• Fraction Lotto
• Fraction Stax™
• Funtastic Frogs
• Let's Look Puzzle Books
• Literacy Kit
• Pizza Party
• Rol 'n' Write Numerals
• Time Dominoes
• Time Snap
• *Speed-Up!: A Kinaesthetic Approach to
  Handwriting* by Lois Addy
• Trigo Pencil Grips
• *Write from the Start* by Teodorescu, I.
  and Addy, L. M.

**NASEN (National Association for
Special Educational Needs)**
4/5 Amber Business Village
Amker Close
Tamworth B77 4RP
Tel: 01827 311500
www.nasen.org.uk

National Literacy Association
Office No.1, The Magistrates' Court
Bargates
Christchurch
Dorset BH23 1PY
Tel: 01202 484079/89
www.nla.org.uk

Network 81
1–7 Woodfield Terrace
Chapel Hill
Stansted
Essex CM24 8AJ
Tel: 01279 627415
www.network81.co.uk
For independent advice re special
educational needs.

**The Nuffield Hearing and Speech
Centre**
The Royal National Ear, Nose and
Throat Hospital
Grays Inn Road
London WC1X 8DA
Tel: 020 7915 1300 or 020 7838 8855
(extension 4158)
www.libraries.islington.gov.uk
Publishes the Nuffield Centre
Dyspraxia Programme, a speech and
language resource.
Assesses children with speech,
language and hearing impairments up
to school leaving age.

Parentline
Endway House
Endway
Hadley
Essex SS7 2AN
Tel: 01702 554782
Helpline: 0808 800222
Organisation for parents under stress.

Parents for Inclusion
Unit 2
70 South Lambeth Road
London SW8 1RL
Helpline: 020 7582 5008
www.parentsforinclusion.org

Puzzle Castle
Susannah Leigh (1994)
Usborne Publishing Ltd
Online from Amazon Books
www.amazon.co.uk

Rainbow People
www.eichild.com
E-mail: environments@eichild.com

**REACH (National Advice Centre for
Children with Reading Difficulties)**
California Country Park
Nine Mile Ride
Finchamstead
Berkshire RG40 4HT
Tel: 0118 973 7575
Helpline: 0845 6040414
www.reach-reading.demon.co.uk

Read and Type a Gift for Life
Mayhew, P. (1997) Gift for Life
Publications
17, Chalky Copse
Hook
Hants RG27 9PX

The Ring Pen
Perfect Pens
94 High Street
Sutton Veny
Warminister
Wiltshire BA12 7AW

Stop and Go Paper
Taskmaster Ltd
Morris Road
Leicester LE2 6BR
Tel: 0116 270 4286

Take Time
Movement exercises for parent, teachers and therapists of children with difficulties in speaking, reading, writing and spelling, 4th edition, Stourbridge, Robinswood Press
South Avenue
Stourbridge
West Midlands DY8 3XY
Tel: 01384 397475

Therapeutic Putty
Trimilin (UK) Ltd
Unit 16
St James Industrial Estate
Westhampnett Road
Chichester
West Sussex P019 4JU
Tel: 01243 784488
www.trimilin.com/hand2002/hand

Tools for Teachers™
Henry OT Services Inc
PO Box 145 Youngtown
AZ 85363-0145
www.ehandprints.com
E-mail: rick@henryot.com

Where's Wally?
Wright, R. and Handford, M., Walker Books
Available online through Amazon Books

Write Angle: The Desktop Writing Aid
Philip and Tacey Ltd
North Way
Andover
Hampshire SP10 5BA
Tel: 01264 332171
E-mail: sales@philip&tacey.co.uk

Write Dance
Ragnhild Oussoren
Lucky Duck Publishing Ltd
3 Thorndale Mews
Bristol BS8 2HX
Tel: 08700 109077
E-mail publishing @luckyduck.co.uk

The Writing and Computers Association
Department of Education,
Taylor Building,
King's College,
University of Aberdeen,
Aberdeen AB9 2UB,
E-mail: k.thomson@aberdeen.ac.uk

References

Addy, L. M. (1996a) A Multiprofessional approach to the treatment of developmental coordination disorder, in *British Journal of Therapy and Rehabilitation*, 3(11).

Addy, L. M. (1996b) *Unlocking the Will to learn: A Study of the Learning Style of Children with and without Dyspraxia*. www.letmelearn.org

Addy, L. M. (2004) *Speed Up! A Kinaesthetic Approach to Handwriting*, Cambridge: LDA Ltd.

Ainscow, M. (1996) The development of inclusive practices in an English primary school: constraints and influences. Paper presented at the American Educational Research Association conference, New York: April 1996.

American Psychiatric Association (APA) (1994) *Diagnostic and Statistical Manual of Mental Disorders*, 4th edition, Washington, DC: APA.

Arnott, M., Gray, J., James, M., Rudduck, J. and Duveen, G. (1998) *Recent Research on Gender and Educational Performance*. (OfSTED Reviews of Research Series). London: The Stationery Office.

Association of Science Education www.ase.org.uk

Ayres, A. J. (1979) *Sensory Intergration and the Child*, California: Western Psychological Services.

Ayres, A. J., Mailloux, Z. and Wendler, C. L. (1987) Developmental Dyspraxia: Is it a Unitary Function? *Occupational Therapy Journal of Research* 7: 93–110.

BBC News Online Network (1999) *Education: 3Rs 'creating couch potatoes'* published Saturday 21 August 1999. Accessed online July 2003 http://news.bbc.co.uk

Bissell, J., Fisher, J., Owens, C. and Polcyn, P. (1998) *Sensory Motor Handbook: A Guide for Implementing and Modifying Activities in the Classroom*, San Antonio, Texas: Therapy Skill Builders.

Black, K. and Haskins, D. (1996) Including all children in TOP PLAY and BT TOP SPORT. *British Journal of Physical Education*, Primary PE focus, winter edition, 9–11.

Booth, G., McDuell, B. and Sears, J. (2000) *World of Science-Special Needs (SEN)*, Copymasters, Oxford University Press.

Booth, T. and Ainscow, M. (2002) *Index for Inclusion Developing Learning and Participation in Schools*, UK: CSIE.

Brooks-Gunn, J., Liaw, F. W. and Klebanov, P. K. (1992) Effects of early intervention on cognitive function of low birth weight preterm infants, *The Journal of Paediatrics* March 120(3): 350–9.

Chia, S. H., Gabriel, H. and St. John, C. (1996) *Sensory Motor Activities for Early Development*, Speechmark Publishing Ltd.

Chinn, S. J. (1998) *Sum Hope: How to Break the Number Barrier*, Souvenir Press.

Chinn, S. J. and Ashcroft, J. R. (1993) *Mathematics for Dyslexics: A Teaching Handbook*, London: Whurr Publishers.

Chu, S. (1991) Occupational Therapy and Sensory Integration, in The Dyspraxia Trust, *Praxis Makes Perfect*, pp. 17–23.

Chu, S. (1995) Helping children with developmental dyspraxia – the role of occupational therapy, lecture notes: unpublished.

Combs, M. L. and Slaby, D. A. (1977) Social skills training with children, in Lahey, B. and Kazdin, A. E. *Advances in Clinical Child Psychology*, New York: Plenum Press.

Daines, B., Flemming, P. and Miller, C. (1996) *Speech and Language Difficulties*, NASEN Publications.

Daly, S. (1992) Understanding Dyspraxia, in *Nursing Times*, 88(30), 22 July 1992.

Denckla, M. B. (1984) *Developmental Dyspraxia. The Clumsy Child*, in Levine, M. D. and Satz, P. *Middle Childhood: Development and Dysfunction*, Boston: University Park Press.

Department for Education (DFE) (1995) *Art in the National Curriculum*, London: HMSO.

Department for Education and Employment (DfEE) (1999) *The National Numeracy Strategy*, DfEE, Cambridge: Cambridge University Press.

Department for Education and Employment (DfEE) (1999) *Physical Education: The National Curriculum for England*, online version. www.nc.uk.net

Department for Education and Skills (2001) *Special Educational Needs Code of Practice*, DfES Publications.

Education Guardian. co.UK Tuesday, 24 September 2002: www.education.guardian.co.uk (accessed 16 July 2003).

Edwards, R., Williams, A. and Baggaley, P. (1993) *Number Activities and Games*, Tamworth, Staffs: NASEN Publications.

El-Naggar, O. (1996) *Specific Learning Difficulties in Mathematics – A Classroom Approach*, Tamworth, Staffs: NASEN.

Feshbach, N. D., Feshbach, S., Fauvre, M. and Ballard-Campbell, M. (1983) *Learning to Care*, Glenview, IL: Scott, Foresman and Co.

Forrester, M. A. (1992) *The Development of Young Children's Social–Cognitive Skills*, Hove: Lawrence Erlbaum Ass.

Frostig, M. (1973) *Frostig Program for the Development of Visual Perception*, Chicago: Follett Publ. Co.

Geary, D. C. (1990) A componential analysis of early learning deficits in mathematics, *Journal of Experimental Psychology* 49: 363–83.

Goddard, S. (1996) *A Teacher's Window into the Child's Mind*, Ridge Press.

Godfrey, K. (1994) Clumsy, Not Clots, in *She* August, p. 183.

Hall, C. (1994) Clumsiness in children 'a medical condition', in *Independent*, 13 January, p. 12.

Haseltine, E. (1999) Brain Works: Your better half, *Discover* 112, June.

Hatch-Rasmussen, C. (1995) *Sensory Integration*, http://www.autism.org/si.html

Henderson, A. (1998) *Maths for the Dyslexic: Practical Guide*, London: David Fulton Publishers.

Henderson, S. E., Dubowitz, L. and Jongmans, M. (1994) Studying 'clumsiness' in preterm children. What Can we Learn? *Midline*, November.

Hughes, S., Kolstad, R. and Briggs, L. D. (1997) Dyscalculia and mathematics achievement, *Journal of Instructional Psychology* 21(1): 64–7.

Hulme, C. and Lord, R. (1986) Clumsy children – a review of recent research, in *Childcare, Health and Development* vol. 12, pp. 257–69.

Inclusive Science and Special Educational Needs (ISSEN) www.issen.org.uk

Johnston, C. A. (1996) *Unlocking the Will to Learn*, Sage: Corwin Press.

Joint Forum for GCSE and GCE (1999) *Candidates with Special Assessment Needs: Special Arrangements and Special Considerations: Regulations and Guidance*, Manchester: Joint Forum.

Kirby, A. (1999) *Dyspraxia. The Hidden Handicap*, Souvenir Press (E & A) Ltd.

Kosc, L. (1974) Developmental Dyscalculia, *Journal of Learning Disabilities* 7(33): 46–59.

Laszlo, J. I. (1983) Perceptuo-motor dysfunction. A research project. Research notes: Unpublished.

Laszlo, J. I. and Bairstow, P. J. (1984) Handwriting difficulties and possible solutions, *School Psychology International* 5: 207–13.

Laszlo, J. I. and Bairstow, P. J. (1985) *Perceptual–motor Behaviour: Developmental Assessment and Therapy*, London: Holt.

Leiderman, J. and Coryell, J. (1982) The origin of left-hand preference: pathological and non-pathological influences, *Neuropsychologia* 20(6): 721–5.

Lomas, J. and Lacey, P. (1993) *Support Services and the Curriculum: A Practical Guide to Collaboration*, London: David Fulton Publishers.

Losse, A., Henderson, S., Elliman, D., Knight, E. and Jongmans, M. (1991) Clumsiness in children – do they grow out of it? A ten-year follow-up study, *Developmental Medicine and Child Neurology* 33: 55–68.

McCartney, G. and Hepper, P. (1999) Development of lateralised behaviour in the human fetus from 12 to 27 weeks gestation, *Developmental Medicine and Child Neurology* 41(2): 83–6 (February).

McKinlay, I. (1996) *Introduction to Dyspraxia*, Dyspraxia Foundation.

McKinlay, I. and Gordon, N. (1989) *Helping Clumsy Children*, United Kingdom: Churchill Livingstone.

McPhillips, M., Hepper, P. G. and Milhern, G. (2000) Effects of replicating primary–reflex movements on specific reading difficulties in children, *Lancet* 355: 537–41.

Maeland, A. and Sovik, N. (1993) Children with motor coordination problems and learning disabilities in reading, spelling, writing and arithmetic, in *European Journal of Special Needs Education* 8(2): 81–98.

Maines, B. and Robinson, G. (1988) *B/G-STEEM: A Self-esteem Scale with Locus of Control Items*, Lucky Duck Publishing Ltd.

Marks, K. (1994), The 'hidden' disorder of a clumsy child, in *Daily Telegraph*, 13 January, p. 16.

Mayhew, P. (1997) *Read and Type a Gift for Life*, Gift for Life Publications.

Montis, K. K. (2000) Language development and concept flexibility in dyscalculia: a case study, *Journal for Learning in Mathematics Education* 31(5): 541–56.

Morley, M. E., Court, D. and Miller, H. (1954) Developmental dysarthria, *British Medical Journal* 1:8.

National Curriculum Council (1991) *Science and Pupils with Special Educational Needs: A workshop Pack for Key Stages 1 and 2*, York: National Curriculum Council.

National Curriculum Council (1992) *Teaching Science to Pupils with Special Educational Needs*, York: National Curriculum Council.

Padsman, J. W., Rotteveel, J. J. and Maassen, B. (1998) Neurodevelopmental profile in low-risk preterm infants at 5 years of age, *European Journal of Paediatric Neurology* 2(1): 7–17.

Parkin, S. and Padley, M. (1986) *Working with Clumsy Children: A Practical Approach for Teachers*, Sheffield: Sheffield Education Department.

Penso, D. (1999) Keyboarding Skills for Children with Disabilities, Whurr Publications.

Peter, M. (1996a) *Art for All-I The Framework*, London: David Fulton Publishers.

Peter, M. (1996b) *Art for All-II the Practice*, London: David Fulton Publishers.

Piek, J. P. and Edwards, K. (1997) The identification of children with developmental coordination disorder by class and physical education teachers, *British Journal of Educational Psychology* 67: 55–67.

Portwood, M. (1996) *Developmental Dyspraxia: A Practical Manual for Parents and Professionals*, Durham: Educational Psychology Service.

Portwood, M. (2002) Research into dyspraxia and DCD, published during 2000–02, in *Dyspraxia Foundation Professional Journal*, Issue 1.

Poustie, J. (1997) *Solutions for Specific Learning Difficulties*, United Kingdom: A Next Generation Publication.

Pressley, M. and McCormick, C. B. (1995) *Advanced Educational Psychology*, New York: HarperCollins.

Qualifications and Curriculum Authority and Department for Education and Employment (2000) *A Scheme of Work for Physical Education*, London: Qualifications and Curriculum Authority.

Quinn, P. O. and Stern, J. M. (1993) *The 'Putting on the Brakes' Activity Book for young people with ADHD*, Washington, DC: Magination Press.

Reeves, D. (1996) *Developmental Verbal Dyspraxia*, information for parents from AFASIC.

Rourke, B. P. and Conway, J. A. (1997) Disabilities of arithmetic and mathematical reasoning: perspectives from neurology and neuropsychology, *Journal of Learning Disabilities* 30(1): 34–46.

Saracho, O. N. (1997) *Teachers' and Students' Cognitive Styles in Early Childhood Education*, Greenwood Press.

Sassoon, R. (1990) *Handwriting: The Way to Teach It*, Cheltenham: Stanley Thornes.

Sassoon, R. (1999) *Handwriting in the Twentieth Century*, London: Routledge.

Schoemaker, M. M. (1993) The effects of physiotherapy on clumsy children's drawing, *Handwriting Review* 55–62.

Sears, C. J. (1986) Mathematics for the learning disabled child in the regular classroom, *Arithmetic Teacher* 1: 5–11.

Senzer, B. (2001) *Dyscalculia: A brief overview* accessed online http://rivermall.com/math/dyscalcr.htm

Sharma, M. C. and Loveless, E. J. (1986) Basic forms of developmental dyscalculia, *Focus on Learning Problems in Mathematics* 8: 55–61.

Sheridan, M., Frost, M. and Sharma, A. (1997) *From Birth to 5 years: Children's Developmental Progress*, London: Routledge Press.

Spiers, P. A. (1987) Acalculia revisited, in Deloche, G. and Seron, P. A. (eds) *Mathematical Disabilities: A Cognitive Neuropschological Perspective*, Hillside: New Jersey.

Stackhouse, J. (1992) Developmental verbal dyspraxia: a review and critique, *European Journal of Disorders of Communication* 27(1): 19–34.

Stackhouse, J. (1992) Developmental Verbal Dyspraxia: A Longitudinal Case Study, in Campbell, R. (ed.) *Mental Lives: Case Studies in Cognition*, Oxford: Blackwell.

Stansfields, J. (1997) *A First Handbook of IT and Special Educational Needs*, Tamworth: NASEN.

Sugden, D. (1991) PE: movement in the right direction, *British Journal of Education* 18(4): 134–6.

Sugden, D. and Chambers, M. (1998) Intervention approaches and children with developmental coordination disorder, *Pediatric Rehabilitation*, 2(4): 139–47.

Teodorescu, I. and Addy, L. M. (1996) *Write from the Start: A Perceptual–Motor Approach to Handwriting*, Cambridge: LDA Ltd.

Thomas, G. (1997) Inclusive schools for an inclusive society, *British Journal of Special Education* 24(3): 103–7.

Vail, P. L. (1993) *Learning Styles*. Rosemont, NJ: Modern Learning Press.

Westwood, P. (1997) *Commonsense Methods for Children with Special Needs*, 3rd edition, London: Routledge.

Williams, S. P. (2002) Developmental verbal dyspraxia – a review. *Dyspraxia Foundation Professional Journal*, Issue 1: 24–30.

Yeo, S. (2002) *Dyslexia, Dyspraxia and Maths*, London: Whurr Publications.

Index